Fundamentals of Individual Tax Preparation
(Includes pointers in the TCJA tax reform)

Study Guide

Prepared and compiled by

FEREY KIAN

American Business GPS

Tax Training Camp

2012 Hollywood Blvd. Ste B., Hollywood, FL 33020

All Rights Reserved

ISBN: 978-1-7322401-7-9

2018©Kian Finance Education and Training Center

www.fkianfa.com

Kian Finance Authority Central Offices located in

2012 Hollywood Blvd. Ste B

Hollywood, FL 33020

954-399-8980

fkianfa@gmail.com

IRS-APPROVED CONTINUING EDUCATION PROVIDER

All rights reserved. No part of this material may be copied, reprinted, reproduced, transmitted or stored in a retrieval system without written permission of Kian Finance Authority Education and Training Center.

The information provided in this Study Guide is, to the best of Kian Finance Authority Tax Education Camp knowledge, believed to be current and accurate; however, Kian Finance Authority is not engaged in rendering legal or other professional advice. Kian Finance Authority Tax Education Camp courses and publications are not substitute for seeking legal, professional advice or conducting individual research. Kian Finance Authority disclaims any responsibility for any adverse consequence resulting from your failure to seek legal or professional advice.

We gratefully acknowledge:

Most of the questions, problems and examples are taken right out of the IRS website, publications, circulars and the following publications. This educational guide was not as thought-provoking without their help.

Unit 1.1: Preliminary Work and Individual Taxpayer Data
IRS publication 1040, Publication 17, *Your Federal Income Tax,*
AFTR guidelines by IRS 2017
Cornell Law School for Section 199A
Trump/GOP Tax Law, Ferey Kian 2018

Look for the legends below to help you remember key points as well as examples, and keywords

Remember this!

Examples

Keywords

Table of Contents

Introduction

This book is a general foundation of individual tax preparation to be used as concise study guide to simplify and highlight the most important parts of the Form 1040.

If there's one advantage to this book, it's how you can become a tax professional buy understanding the concepts instead of entering data in tax software. If you have worked with QuickBooks, you know what I'm saying. The software does everything so you don't have to know anything, just like our smart phones.

The goal in this book is to help you sit on the driver seat and to prepare taxes without any forms and even on a napkin. Some of the numbers will change in years because they are indexed for inflation (usually by $50 a year. Penalties may rise by 2-4% rounded up to $5-$10). With the same token, mileage rates are mostly tied to gas prices for now until we get a more environmentally suitable fuel and then the mileage rate will be based on other factors. The basics are always constant.

As we've seen in the TCJA (Tax Reforms of 2017), some numbers may change, such as Child Tax Credit which became a refundable credit, or the new 20% deduction on pass-thru income, but remember, the fundamentals always remain the same, and this book is only focused on those concepts that don't change in the individual tax preparation.

As years go by, and numbers change, check our website at fkianfa.com/updates as a sort of companion to this book. Here's the link: http://fkianfa.com/newsletter/

This study guide is written based on my students' questions, mix-ups and headaches. It uses the simplest way to help you navigate and understand the confusing sites out there. As you may have noticed, the IRS website is like an ocean of information. If someone dropped you in the middle, you wouldn't know what direction to swim to safety. This book is your GPS. You will know how to find the information you need instead of going thru hundreds of sites.

As a next step, you may want to become specialized in one of the income areas such as Foreign Income, Schedule B, or D. I would also suggest embarking on Business Tax Preparation which provides a higher fee in your business.

To set a goal for yourself, also look into the Enrolled Agent designation where a lucrative career is eagerly expecting you. It's like having a law degree or CPA credential as far as the IRS is concerned.

Good luck with whatever you do and enjoy your first step in becoming a tax professional who goes beyond data entry for a software company.

Ferey Kian, EA
Hollywood, Florida
July 2017

What Forms Should I Use (Prior toTCJA)?

Use 1040EZ if...

1. Single or married filing jointly.
2. No dependents.
3. No adjustments to income.
4. Claim only Earned income credit
5. Under 65
6. Income is less than $100,000.
7. Your taxable interest was not over $1,500.
8. No 1040EZ if Head of Household or married filing separately, IRA distribution, Rent, education credit.

Use 1040 A if...

1- Your income came from one these sources.
  – Wages, salaries, tips.
  – Interest and ordinary dividends.
  – Capital gain distributions.
2. You can claim:
  – Educator expenses.
  – IRA deduction.
  – Student loan interest deduction
  – Tuition and fees deduction
3. Your taxable income is less than $100,000.
4. No self-employment income, rent-Royalty, alimony, Sch. A. items

Other popular forms:
- **Form 1040-C is** used by aliens who intend to leave the United States or any of its possessions
- **File Form 1040NR** nonresident alien engaged in a trade or business in the United States
- Form 1040X to correct Forms 1040, 1040A, 1040EZ-T, 1040NR, or 1040NR-EZ.
- **Form 1041 Decedent's Estate**
- **Everyone else will use Form 1040. This form is also by tax professionals. Can you guess why?**

Who is a Resident?
- Green card
- Meet 183 day presence test
- (31 day of current year, previous year's day is 1/3 of a day, two years ago, each day is considered 1/6 of a day.)
- Commuting days not counted.(say from Mexico and Canada)
- Have your tax home in the foreign country if you don't meet the 183 day

If you are an alien staying because of school, teaching, athletic activities, etc. This does not qualify as residence

Main segments you need to remember with your eyes wide shut:

1-Biographical Information, 2- Filing Status, 3-Dependent, 4 Income, 5 Adjustments

And at the bottom of the page one of 1040, line 37 here in 2017 form, you see the most important number: AGI. Everything after this in the form depends on this number.

AGI minus Deductions (standard or Itemized), minus Exemptions, gives you the Taxable Income. But Still you can reduce this tax liability with some credits. See if these are applicable to you or your clients

Tax and Credits	38	Amount from line 37 (adjusted gross income)		38	
	39a	Check if: ☐ **You** were born before January 2, 1950, ☐ Blind. ☐ **Spouse** was born before January 2, 1950, ☐ Blind. } Total boxes checked ▶ 39a			
	b	If your spouse itemizes on a separate return or you were a dual-status alien, check here▶	39b☐		
Standard Deduction for— • People who check any box on line 39a or 39b or who can be claimed as a dependent, see instructions. • All others: Single or Married filing separately, $6,200 Married filing jointly or Qualifying widow(er), $12,400 Head of household, $9,100	40	**Itemized deductions** (from Schedule A) or your **standard deduction** (see left margin)		40	
	41	Subtract line 40 from line 38		41	
	42	Exemptions. If line 38 is $152,525 or less, multiply $3,950 by the number on line 6d. Otherwise, see instructions		42	
	43	**Taxable income.** Subtract line 42 from line 41. If line 42 is more than line 41, enter -0-		43	
	44	Tax (see instructions). Check if any from: a ☐ Form(s) 8814 b ☐ Form 4972 c ☐		44	
	45	Alternative minimum tax (see instructions). Attach Form 6251		45	
	46	Excess advance premium tax credit repayment. Attach Form 8962		46	
	47	Add lines 44, 45, and 46 ▶		47	
	48	Foreign tax credit. Attach Form 1116 if required	48		
	49	Credit for child and dependent care expenses. Attach Form 2441	49		
	50	Education credits from Form 8863, line 19	50		
	51	Retirement savings contributions credit. Attach Form 8880	51		
	52	Child tax credit. Attach Schedule 8812, if required	52		
	53	Residential energy credits. Attach Form 5695	53		
	54	Other credits from Form: a ☐ 3800 b ☐ 8801 c ☐	54		
	55	Add lines 48 through 54. These are your **total credits**		55	
	56	Subtract line 55 from line 47. If line 55 is more than line 47, enter -0- ▶		56	
Other Taxes	57	Self-employment tax. Attach Schedule SE		57	
	58	Unreported social security and Medicare tax from Form: a ☐ 4137 b ☐ 8919		58	
	59	Additional tax on IRAs, other qualified retirement plans, etc. Attach Form 5329 if required		59	
	60a	Household employment taxes from Schedule H		60a	
	b	First-time homebuyer credit repayment. Attach Form 5405 if required		60b	
	61	Health care: individual responsibility (see instructions) Full-year coverage ☐		61	
	62	Taxes from: a ☐ Form 8959 b ☐ Form 8960 c ☐ Instructions; enter code(s)		62	
	63	Add lines 56 through 62. This is your **total tax** ▶		63	
Payments If you have a qualifying child, attach Schedule EIC.	64	Federal income tax withheld from Forms W-2 and 1099	64		
	65	2014 estimated tax payments and amount applied from 2013 return	65		
	66a	**Earned income credit (EIC)**	66a		
	b	Nontaxable combat pay election	66b		
	67	Additional child tax credit. Attach Schedule 8812	67		
	68	American opportunity credit from Form 8863, line 8	68		
	69	Net premium tax credit. Attach Form 8962	69		
	70	Amount paid with request for extension to file	70		
	71	Excess social security and tier 1 RRTA tax withheld	71		
	72	Credit for federal tax on fuels. Attach Form 4136	72		
	73	Credits from Form: a ☐ 2439 b ☐ Reserved c ☐ Reserved d ☐	73		
	74	Add lines 64, 65, 66a, and 67 through 73. These are your **total payments** ▶		74	
Refund Direct deposit? See instructions.	75	If line 74 is more than line 63, subtract line 63 from line 74. This is the amount you **overpaid**		75	
	76a	Amount of line 75 you want **refunded to you.** If Form 8888 is attached, check here ▶ ☐		76a	
	▶ b	Routing number ▶ c Type: ☐ Checking ☐ Savings			
	▶ d	Account number			
	77	Amount of line 75 you want **applied to your 2015 estimated tax** ▶	77		
Amount You Owe	78	**Amount you owe.** Subtract line 74 from line 63. For details on how to pay, see instructions ▶		78	
	79	Estimated tax penalty (see instructions)	79		

Third Party Designee Do you want to allow another person to discuss this return with the IRS (see instructions)? ☐ **Yes. Complete below.** ☐ **No**

Designee's name ▶ ___ Phone no. ▶ ___ Personal identification number (PIN) ▶ ☐☐☐☐☐

Sign Here
Joint return? See instructions.
Keep a copy for your records.

Under penalties of perjury, I declare that I have examined this return and accompanying schedules and statements, and to the best of my knowledge and belief, they are true, correct, and complete. Declaration of preparer (other than taxpayer) is based on all information of which preparer has any knowledge.

Your signature	Date	Your occupation	Daytime phone number
Spouse's signature. If a joint return, **both** must sign.	Date	Spouse's occupation	If the IRS sent you an Identity Protection PIN, enter it here (see inst.) ☐☐☐☐☐☐

Paid Preparer Use Only

Print/Type preparer's name	Preparer's signature	Date	Check ☐ if self-employed	PTIN
Firm's name ▶			Firm's EIN ▶	
Firm's address ▶			Phone no.	

Form **1040** (2014)

A draft of 2018 form is attached only to show the reserved sections and the forms are developed by the IRS:

	1	Wages, salaries, tips, etc. Attach Form(s) W-2			1	
Attach Form(s) W-2. Also attach Form(s) W-2G and 1099-R if tax was withheld.	2a	Tax-exempt interest . . .	2a		b Taxable interest . . .	2b	
	3a	Qualified dividends . . .	3a		b Ordinary dividends . . .	3b	
	4a	IRAs, pensions, and annuities .	4a		b Taxable amount . . .	4b	
	5a	Social security benefits . .	5a		b Taxable amount . . .	5b	
	6	Total income. Add lines 1 through 5. Add any amount from Schedule 1, line 22			6	
	7	Adjusted gross income. If you have no adjustments to income, enter the amount from line 6; otherwise, subtract Schedule 1, line 36, from line 6			7	

Standard Deduction for—
- Single or married filing separately, $12,000
- Married filing jointly or Qualifying widow(er), $24,000
- Head of household, $18,000
- If you checked any box under Standard deduction, see instructions.

8	Standard deduction or itemized deductions (from Schedule A)	8
9	Qualified business income deduction (see instructions)	9
10	Taxable income. Subtract lines 8 and 9 from line 7. If zero or less, enter -0- . .	10
11	a Tax (see inst) _____ (check if any from: 1 ☐ Form(s) 8814 2 ☐ Form 4972 3 ☐ _____)	
	b Add any amount from Schedule 2 and check here . . . . ▶ ☐	11
12	a Child tax credit/credit for other dependents _____ b Add any amount from Schedule 3 and check here ▶ ☐	12
13	Subtract line 12 from line 11. If zero or less, enter -0-	13
14	Other taxes. Attach Schedule 4	14
15	Total tax. Add lines 13 and 14	15
16	Federal income tax withheld from Forms W-2 and 1099	16
17	Refundable credits: a EIC (see inst.) _____ b Sch 8812 _____ c Form 8863 _____	
	Add any amount from Schedule 5 _____	17
18	Add lines 16 and 17. These are your total payments	18

Refund

19	If line 18 is more than line 15, subtract line 15 from line 18. This is the amount you **overpaid** . . .	19
20a	Amount of line 19 you want **refunded to you**. If Form 8888 is attached, check here . . . ▶ ☐	20a

Direct deposit? ▶ See instructions.
b Routing number ☐☐☐☐☐☐☐☐☐ ▶ c Type: ☐ Checking ☐ Savings
▶ d Account number ☐☐☐☐☐☐☐☐☐

21	Amount of line 19 you want **applied to your 2019 estimated tax** . . ▶	21

Amount You Owe

22	**Amount you owe.** Subtract line 18 from line 15. For details on how to pay, see instructions . . . ▶	22
23	Estimated tax penalty (see instructions) . . . . ▶	23

Go to *www.irs.gov/Form1040* for instructions and the latest information.   Form **1040** (201

DRAFT AS OF August 13, 2018 DO NOT FILE

The Tax Reform Bill tries to shorten the tax forms and particularly 1040 to a postcard, but as you can see above, still business tax, rental or several credits are not yet worked out in the form. Let's wish them the best of luck, because we always should try to simplify things.

Section I: IRS TAX PREPARER REQUIREMENTS

"Ask the right questions; get the right answers."

IRS motto

Due Diligence Starts Here.....

Chapter I: Gathering Taxpayer's Data

To prepare an income tax return for a client, these are general steps for your due diligence.

1. Review prior year's return for accuracy, comparison, and carryovers for current year's return.
2. Collect taxpayer's biographical information (e.g., date of birth, age, marital status, citizenship, dependents).
3. Determine filing status.
4. Determine all sources of taxable and non-taxable income (e.g., wages, interest, business, sale of property, dividends, rental income and income from flow-through entities, alimony, government payments, and pension distributions).
5. Determine applicable adjustments to gross income (e.g., self-employed health insurance, self- employment tax, student loan interest deduction, alimony paid, tuition, and fees deduction).
6. Determine standard deduction and Schedule A itemized deductions (e.g., state and local tax, real estate tax, cash contributions, non-cash contributions, unreimbursed employee expense, medical expense, and mortgage interest).
7. Determine applicable credits (e.g., earned income tax credit, child tax credit, education, retirement savings, dependent and child care credit).
8. Understand tax payments (e.g., withholding, estimated payments).
9. Recognize items that will affect future returns (e.g., carryovers and depreciation).
10. Determine special filing requirements (e.g., presidentially declared disaster areas).
11. Determine filing requirements (including extensions and amended returns).
12. Understand due dates, including extensions. 13. Determine personal exemptions, including dependents.
14. Determine qualifying child/relative tests for Earned Income Credit.

Exhibit 1: Double check the spelling and Social Security number for each client

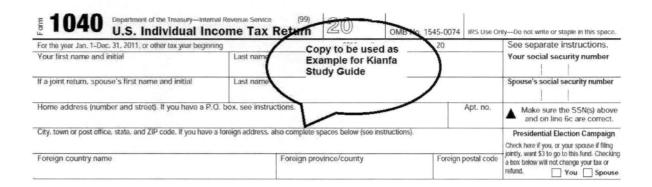

Client's Identity

A Social Security Number is required for the taxpayer, the taxpayer's spouse (if married), and any dependents listed on the tax return. A nonresident alien who is not eligible for a Social Security Number must request an Individual Taxpayer Identification Number. The issuance of an ITIN does not:

- Entitle the recipient to Social Security benefits or the Earned Income Tax Credit
- Create a presumption regarding the individual's immigration status
- Give the individual the right to work in the United States

An ITIN will expire if the ITIN holder didn't file a tax return or wasn't included as a dependent on the tax return of another taxpayer for three consecutive years. In this case, the ITIN will expire on the last day of the third consecutive year.

Any individual who fails to use their assigned ITIN for three consecutive tax years will unfortunately find that their ITIN is no longer valid. He or she will need to apply for a new ITIN before making his or her tax filing.

- ITINs issued in 2009 or in 2010 are valid for tax filing purposes until January 1, 2019.
- ITINs issues during 2011 or 2012 will remain valid until expiring on January 1, 2020.

All individuals who earn income in the US must have valid IDs, Social Security Number or unexpired ITIN number in order to file their tax return.

Taxpayers who cannot obtain an SSN must apply for an ITIN if they file a U.S. tax return or are listed on a tax return as a spouse or dependent. These taxpayers must file **Form W-7,** *Application for Individual Taxpayer Identification Number*, and supply documentation that will establish foreign status and true identity.

Adopted children may be claimed as dependents even if they do not have a Social Security Number yet. If the taxpayer is unable to secure a Social Security Number for a child until the adoption is final, he may request an Adoption Taxpayer Identification Number (ATIN).

The ATIN may NOT be used in order to claim the Earned Income Credit. A taxpayer should apply for an ATIN only if he or she is adopting a child *and also* meets all of the following qualifications.

- The child is legally placed in the taxpayer's home for legal adoption.
- The adoption is a domestic adoption OR the adoption is a legal foreign adoption and the child has a Permanent Resident Alien Card or Certificate of Citizenship.
- The taxpayer cannot obtain the child's existing SSN even though she has made a reasonable attempt to obtain it from the birth parents, the placement agency, and other persons.
- The taxpayer cannot obtain an SSN for the child from the Social Security Administration for any reason (for example, the adoption is not final).
- Administration for any reason (for example, the adoption is not final).

An ATIN can be requested for an adopted child using IRS **Form W-7A,** *Application for Taxpayer Identification Number for Pending U.S. Adoptions.* Generally, anyone who files a tax return or claims a dependent must have a Taxpayer Identification Number: either an ITIN, ATIN, or an SSN.

***Exception*: A Child Who was Born and Died in the Same Tax Year

Note: If a primary taxpayer, spouse, or both have ITINs, they are ineligible to receive the Earned Income Tax Credit (EITC), even if their dependents have valid

SSNs. If the taxpayer and spouse (if filing jointly) have valid SSNs, only dependents with valid SSNs – not ITINs – qualify to receive EITC.

Filing Status

In order to file a tax return, a tax preparer must identify the taxpayer's filing status. There are five filing statuses, and you must clearly understand the rules governing each status. There are also special rules that you must know regarding annulled marriages and widows/widowers.

Exhibit 2: Filing status

1. Single

A taxpayer is considered **Single** if, on the last day of the tax year, the taxpayer was either:

- Unmarried
- Legally separated or divorced
- Widowed (and not remarried during the year)

Although a taxpayer is considered **Single**, the taxpayer may qualify for another filing status that gives her a lower tax, such as Head of Household or Qualifying Widow(er).

A taxpayer who is single (or legally divorced) on the *last* day of the year is considered **Single** for the *entire* tax year. A taxpayer is also "considered unmarried" if, on the last day of the tax year, she is legally separated from her spouse under a divorce decree or separate maintenance decree.

 Example:
Ross and Jennifer legally divorced on December 31, 2015. Ross and Jennifer do not have any dependents. They each must file SINGLE for tax year 2015. They may NOT file a joint return for 2015.

State law governs whether a person is considered *married* or *legally separated*. If a taxpayer is legally divorced on the last day of the year, she is considered single for the whole year. Divorced taxpayers CANNOT choose "Married Filing Jointly" as their filing status.

 Special Note - Annulled Marriages (Single): If a marriage is annulled, then the marriage is considered *never to have existed*. Annulment is a legal procedure for declaring a marriage null and void. Unlike a divorce, an annulment is *retroactive*. If a taxpayer obtains a court decree of annulment that holds that no valid marriage ever existed, the couple is considered unmarried even if they filed joint returns for earlier years.

Taxpayers who have annulled their marriage must file amended returns (**Form 1040X**) claiming Single (or Head of Household status, if applicable) for all the tax years affected by the annulment that are not closed by the statute of limitations. The statute of limitations for filing generally does not expire until *three years* after an original return was filed.

> **Example:**
> Sarah and Robert were granted an annulment on October of the tax year. They were married for two years. They do not have any dependents. They must each file **Single** for this year and the prior two years tax returns must be amended to reflect **Single** as their filing status.

Married taxpayers may file jointly even if one spouse did not earn any income. Taxpayers may use the **Married Filing Jointly (MFJ)** status if they are married and either:

- They live together as husband and wife
- They live apart but are not legally separated or divorced
- They are separated under an interlocutory (not final) divorce decree
- The taxpayer's spouse died during the year and the taxpayer has not remarried

For federal tax purposes, a "marriage" only qualifies for joint filing status if the marriage is between a man and a woman. Although many states now offer same-sex unions, they are not recognized for federal tax purposes. The IRS will recognize a common law marriage if it is recognized by the state where the taxpayers now live or where the common law marriage began.

2. Married Filing Jointly (MFJ)

On a joint return, spouses report combined income and deduct combined allowable expenses. Spouses can file a joint return even if only one spouse had income. Both spouses must include all of their income, exemptions, and deductions on their joint return. Both husband and wife must agree to sign the return, and are responsible for any tax owed. Both spouses may be held responsible for all the tax due, even if all the income was earned by only one spouse. A subsequent divorce usually does not relieve either spouse of the liability associated with the original joint return.

If a taxpayer files a separate return, he may elect to amend the filing status to **Married Filing Jointly** at any time within three years of the due date of the original return. This does not include any extensions. A "separate return" includes a return filed claiming Married Filing Separately (MFS), Single, or Head of Household filing status. Once a taxpayer files a joint return, he cannot choose to file a separate return (**MFS**) for the year *after* the due date of the return. So, for example, if a married couple filed their joint tax 2015 return on March 25, 2016, and one of the spouses decides to file **MFS**, then they only have until April 17, 2016, to elect **MFS** filing status.

If a spouse dies during the year, the couple is still considered married for the whole year and can choose **Married Filing Jointly** as their filing status. In this case, the surviving spouse signs the joint return as the "surviving spouse" on the signature line of Form 1040.

Example:
John and his wife Susan have always filed jointly. Susan dies suddenly this year, and her will names Harriet, her daughter from a previous marriage, as the executor for her estate and all her legal affairs. John files a joint return with Susan this year, but Harriet, as the executor, decides that it would be better for Susan's estate if her tax return was filed **MFS**. Harriet has the right to change Susan's filing status on her tax return to **MFS**. Harriet files an amended return tax year claiming MFS status for Susan, and signs the return as the executor.

---

3. Married Filing Separately (MFS)

The **Married Filing Separately (MFS)** status is for taxpayers who are married and either:

- Choose to file separate returns
- Do not agree to file a joint return

Taxpayers who are married may choose the **Married Filing Separately** status, which means the husband and wife report their own incomes and deductions on separate returns, even if one spouse had no income. A married taxpayer who files separately must write the spouse's name and Social Security Number (or ITIN) on the front of the Form 1040.
If a taxpayer files a separate return, he generally reports only his own income, exemptions, credits, and deductions (although there are special rules in community property states).
Special rules apply to **Married Filing Separately** taxpayers, which usually results in the taxpayer paying a higher tax. For example, when filing separately:

- The tax rate is generally higher than on a joint return, and
- Taxpayers cannot take credits for child and dependent care expenses, earned income, and certain adoption and education expenses.

There are some rare instances when **MFS** might be a more beneficial filing status. There is a potential advantage of using **MFS** status whenever:

- Both spouses have taxable income, and
- At least one (usually the person with the lower income) has high itemized deductions that are limited by Adjusted Gross Income (AGI). For example, it may happen that one spouse has very high medical expenses and the **MFS** filing status will give him a lower taxable income, because the medical expenses would have been "phased out" on a joint return.

One common reason taxpayers file as **Married Filing Separately** is to avoid an offset of their refund against their current spouse's outstanding prior debt. This includes past due child support, past due student loans, or a tax liability a spouse incurred before the marriage.

 Example:

Jerry and Danielle usually file jointly. However, Danielle has chosen to separate her finances from her husband. Jerry wishes to file jointly with Danielle, but she has refused. Danielle files using **Married Filing Separately** as her filing status; therefore, Jerry is forced to file **MFS** as well.

 There are special rules on **MFS** returns regarding itemized deductions. If a married couple files separately and one spouse itemizes their deductions, the other spouse must either:

- Also itemize their deductions
- Claim "0" (zero) as the standard deduction

In other words, a taxpayer whose spouse itemizes deductions cannot take the standard deduction. The question of who is itemizing only becomes a consideration when *both* taxpayers are filing **MFS**. If one spouse qualifies for Head of Household, the fact that the other one is filing **MFS** and is itemizing doesn't apply.

The Basic Rules on an MFS Tax Return

1. The tax rate will generally be higher than it would be on a joint return.
2. The exemption amount for the Alternative Minimum Tax will be half that allowed to a joint return filer.

3. Neither spouse can take the credit for child and dependent care expenses.
4. Neither spouse can take the Earned Income Tax Credit.
5. Taxpayers cannot take the exclusion or credit for adoption expenses in most cases.
6. Neither spouse can take education credits.
7. Neither spouse can exclude any interest from qualified U.S. savings bonds used for higher education expenses.
8. If one spouse itemizes deductions, the other spouse cannot claim the standard deduction, even if he does not have qualified expenses to itemize. If the taxpayers choose to claim the standard deduction, the basic standard deduction is half the amount allowed on a joint return.
9. A taxpayer's capital loss deduction for MFS is $1,500 instead of $3,000 when filing a joint return.
10. A taxpayer cannot roll over amounts from a traditional IRA into a Roth IRA on an MFS return.
11. For calculating the taxable portion of Social Security, the "provisional income amount" is zero (not $25,000 for Single or $32,000 for Married Filing Jointly).

4. Head of Household

Taxpayers may use the **Head of Household (HOH)** status if they meet three criteria:

1. The taxpayer must be "considered unmarried" (single, divorced, or legally separated) on the last day of the year, or meet the tests for married persons living apart with dependent children.
2. The taxpayer must have also paid more than half the cost of maintaining a main home.
3. The taxpayer must have had a qualifying person living in her home *more* than half the year (an exception exists for qualifying parent).

In general, the **Head of Household** status is for unmarried taxpayers who paid *more* than half the cost of keeping up a home for a qualified dependent relative who lived with them in the home more than half the tax year. Valid household expenses include:

- Rent, mortgage interest, real estate taxes
- Home insurance, repairs, utilities
- Domestic help, such as in-home cleaning services and lawn care
- Food eaten in the home

Welfare payments are not considered amounts that the taxpayer provides to maintain a home.

Special Rule - Dependent Parents: If a taxpayer's qualifying person is a dependent *parent*, the taxpayer may still file **Head of Household** even if the parent *does not live* with the taxpayer. The taxpayer must pay more than half the cost of keeping up a home that was the parent's main home for the entire year. A taxpayer also is considered "keeping up a main home" if he pays more than half the cost of keeping his parent in a rest home (Publication 17).

This rule also applies to parents, step-parents, grandparents, etc. who are related to the taxpayer by blood, marriage, or adoption (other examples include step-parents).

*** *Special Rule - Death or Birth during the Year*: A taxpayer may still file as **Head of Household** if the qualifying individual is born (or dies) during the year. The taxpayer must have provided more than half of the cost of keeping up a home that was the individual's main home while the person was alive.

Example:
Tina is single and financially supports her mother Phyllis, who lives in her own apartment. Phyllis dies suddenly on September 15, 2010. Tina may still claim her mother as a dependent and file Head of Household in 2010.

For the purposes of the **Head of Household** filing status, a "qualifying person" is defined as either:

- A qualifying child
- A married child who can be claimed as a dependent
- A dependent parent

The taxpayer's qualifying child includes the taxpayer's child or stepchild (whether by blood or adoption); foster child, sibling, or stepsibling; or a descendant of any of these. For example, a niece or nephew, stepbrother, foster child, or a grandchild may all be eligible as "qualifying persons" for the purpose of the **Head of Household** filing status.

The "qualifying person" for **Head of Household** filing status must always be related to the taxpayer either by blood or marriage (with the exception of a foster child, who also qualifies if the child was legally placed in the home by a government agency or entity).

Example:

Ramon has lived with his girlfriend Deborah and her son Thomas for five years. Ramon pays all of the costs of keeping up their home. Deborah is unemployed and does not contribute to the household costs. Ramon is not related to Thomas and cannot claim him as a dependent. No one else lives in the household. Ramon cannot file as **Head of Household** because neither Deborah nor Thomas is a "qualifying person" for Ramon.

An unrelated individual may still be considered a "qualifying relative" for a dependency exemption, but will NOT be a qualifying person for the **Head of Household** filing status. In the example below, the taxpayer lives with an unrelated person (a friend), who qualifies as his dependent, but since they are unrelated (either by blood or marriage), then the taxpayer cannot claim **Head of Household** filing status.

In order for a taxpayer to file as **Head of Household**, a qualifying child does not have to be a dependent of the taxpayer (unless the qualifying person is married). So, to explain further, a taxpayer may still file as **Head of Household** and NOT claim the qualifying person as his dependent. This happens most often with divorced parents. The example below illustrates a common scenario.

Taxpayers must always specify the qualifying person who makes them eligible for **Head of Household** filing status. If the qualifying person is also the taxpayer's dependent, then the dependent's name is entered on the Form 1040 Exemptions section, (line 6c). If the qualifying person is the taxpayer's child and is NOT a dependent, then the taxpayer must enter the child's name on the return's Filing Status section (Form 1040, line 4).

The Florida Keys
Key West
Close To Perfect - Far From Normal

*** *Special Rules - HOH Married and Living Apart with Dependent Child*: Some married taxpayers who live apart from their spouses and provide for dependent children may be considered "unmarried" for **Head of Household** purposes. These taxpayers are permitted to file as **Head of Household** if they meet all of the following criteria:

- The married taxpayer chooses to not file a joint return with his or her spouse.
- The taxpayer paid more than half the cost of keeping up the qualifying child's home for the year.
- The taxpayer's spouse *did not live in the home* during the last six months of the year.

Example:

Benny and Carol separated in February 2010 and lived apart for the rest of the year. They do not have a written separation agreement and are not divorced yet. Their six-year-old daughter Pauline lived with Benny all year. Benny and Carol will not file a joint tax return. Benny paid more than half the cost of keeping up his home. Benny claims Pauline's exemption because he is the custodial parent. Benny can also claim **Head of Household** status for 2010. Although Benny is still legally married, he can file as **Head of Household** because he meets all the requirements to be "considered unmarried."

The taxpayer's home must be the *main home* of the taxpayer's qualifying child, step-child, or eligible foster child for more than half the year in order to qualify under this special rule for married spouses who are living apart.

The Florida Keys
KeyWest
Close To Perfect · Far From Normal

*** *Special Rule - Nonresident Alien Spouses*: A taxpayer who is married to a *nonresident alien* spouse may elect to file as **Head of Household** even if both spouses lived together throughout the year.

Exemptions	6a	☐ Yourself. If someone can claim you as a dependent, **do not** check box 6a	}	Boxes checked on 6a and 6b
	b	☐ Spouse		No. of children

c	Dependents:	(2) Dependent's social security number	(3) Dependent's relationship to you	(4) ✓ if child under age 17 qualifying for child tax credit (see instructions)	on 6c who: • lived with you
(1) First name	Last name				• did not live with you due to divorce or separation (see instructions)
If more than four dependents, see instructions and check here ► ☐		*Copy to be used as example in Kianfa Study guide*		☐ ☐ ☐ ☐	Dependents on 6c not entered above
	d	Total number of exemptions claimed		Add numbers on lines above ►

Exhibit 3: Note exemptions for dependents, but see Box 4 in Filing Status as well.

Line 4 vs. Line 6

Filing Status	1	☐ Single	**Box 4** ` ` household (with qualifying person). (See instructions.) If
	2	☐ Married filing jointly (even if only one had income)	the qualifying person is a child but not your dependent, enter this
Check only one box.	3	☐ Married filing separately. Enter spouse's SSN above and full name here. ►	child's name here. ► _____
			5 ☐ Qualifying widow(er) with dependent child

Exhibit 4: Box 4 is highlighted

Taxpayers must always specify the qualifying person who makes them eligible for **Head of Household** filing status.

A. If the qualifying person is the taxpayer's child and is NOT a dependent, enter the child's name on the return's Filing Status section (Form 1040, line 4).

24

B.   If the qualifying person is the taxpayer's dependent, then the dependent's name is entered on the Form 1040 Exemptions section (line 6c).

 Example:

George and Florida have been divorced for five years. They have one child, a 12-year-old son named Orlando. Orlando lives with his mother Florida and only sees his father on weekends. Therefore, Florida is the custodial parent. Florida and George have an agreement with each other that allows George to claim the dependency exemption for Orlando on his tax return. In 2010, George correctly files **Single** and claims Orlando as his dependent. Elizabeth may still file as **Head of Household**. There is an area on Form 1040 that allows Elizabeth to indicate **Head of Household** status and supply Orlando's name and Social Security Number.

Caution: The followings only show an overview of the rules. For details, see Publication 17.

- You cannot claim any dependents if you or your spouse, if filing jointly, could be claimed as a dependent by another taxpayer.
- You cannot claim a married person who files a joint return as a dependent unless that joint return is only a claim for a refund and there would be no tax liability for either spouse on separate returns.
- You cannot claim a person as a dependent unless that person is a U.S. citizen, U.S. resident alien, U.S. national, or a resident of Canada or Mexico.
- You cannot claim a person as a dependent unless that person is your *qualifying child* or *qualifying relative*.

 # Qualifying Child of More Than One Person

If a child meets the conditions to be a qualifying child of more than one person, only one person can claim the child as a qualifying child for all of the following tax benefits, unless the special rule for children of divorced or separated parents applies.

6 Benefits of Qualifying Child

1. Dependency Exemption
2. Head of Household
3. Credit for Child and Dependent Care Expenses
   (I told you that this book is a page turner)

4. Child Tax Credit
5. Earned Income Credit
6. Exclusion from income for Dependent Care Benefits

No other person can take any of the six tax benefits listed above unless he or she has a different qualifying child. If you and any person can claim the child as a qualifying child, the following rules apply.

If only one of the persons is the child's parent, the child is treated as the qualifying child of the parent. If the parents do not file a joint return together but both parents claim the child as a qualifying child, *the IRS will treat the child as the qualifying child of the parent with whom the child lived for the longer period of time during the year.*

If the child lived with each parent for the same amount of time, the IRS will treat the child as the qualifying child of the parent who had the higher adjusted gross income (AGI) for the year. If no parent can claim the child as a qualifying child, the child is treated as the qualifying child of the person who had the highest AGI for the year.

If a parent can claim the child as a qualifying child but no parent does, the child is treated as the qualifying child of the person who had the highest AGI for the year, but only if that person's AGI is higher than the highest AGI of any of the child's parents who can claim the child.

 Example:
Your daughter meets the conditions to be a qualifying child for both you and your mother. Under the rules above, you are entitled to treat your daughter as a qualifying child for all of the six tax benefits listed above for which you otherwise would qualify. Your mother is not entitled to take any of the six tax benefits listed above unless she has a different qualifying child. However, if your mother's AGI is higher than yours, you can let your mother treat your daughter as her qualifying child. If you do that, your daughter is not your qualifying child for any of the 6 benefits.

For more details and examples, see Publications 17 and 501.

5. Qualifying Widow/Widower (With a Dependent Child)

This filing status yields a tax rate *equal to* **Married Filing Jointly**. Surviving spouses receive the same standard deduction and tax rates as taxpayers who are **Married Filing Jointly**. In the year of the spouse's death, a taxpayer can file a joint return. For the following two years after death, the surviving spouse can use the **Qualifying Widow(er)** filing status as long as he or she has a qualifying dependent. After two years, the filing status converts to **Single** or **Head of Household**, whichever applies. For example, if the taxpayer's spouse died in 2018 and the surviving spouse did not remarry, he or she can use the **Qualifying Widow(er)** filing status for 2019 and 2020.

 Example:
Barbara and Kenneth are married. Kenneth dies on December 3, 2018. Barbara has one dependent child, a 15-year-old daughter named Hannah. Barbara does not remarry. Therefore, Barbara's filing status for 2008 is **MFJ**. Barbara can file as a **Qualifying Widow** in 2019 and 2020, which is a more favorable filing status than **Single** or **Head of Household**. In 2021, Barbara would qualify for **Head of Household** filing status.

To qualify for the **Qualifying Widow(er)** filing status, the taxpayer must:

- Not have remarried before the end of the tax year
- Have been eligible to file a joint return for the year the spouse died; it does not matter if a joint return was actually filed
- Have a child, step-child, or adopted child who qualifies as the taxpayer's qualifying child for the year
- Have furnished over half the cost of keeping up the child's home for the entire year

Review

Take a moment to review what you have covered in this lesson. The five filing statuses are:

1. Single
2. Married Filing Jointly
3. Married Filing Separately
4. Head of Household
5. Qualifying Widow(er) With Dependent Child

Filing status is used to determine a taxpayer's filing requirements, standard deduction, and eligibility for certain credits and deductions, and the correct tax. If a taxpayer qualifies for more than one filing status, he or she may choose the one that produces a lower tax. If married taxpayers choose to file separately, they must show their spouse's name and Social Security Number on the return.

1. A person's marital status on the *last day of the year* determines the marital status for the entire year.
2. **Single** filing status generally applies to anyone who is unmarried, divorced (or legally separated according to state law).
3. A married couple may elect file a joint return together. Both spouses must agree to file a joint return.
4. If one spouse died during the year, the taxpayer may file a joint return in the year of death.
5. **Head of Household** usually applies to taxpayers who are unmarried. A taxpayer must have paid more than half the cost of maintaining a home for a qualifying person in order to qualify for **HOH**.
6. A widow or widower with one or more dependent children may be able to use the **Qualifying Widow(er) with Dependent Child** filing status, which is only available for two years following the year of the spouse's death.

Chapter II: Filing Requirements for Most Taxpayers

Sometimes, a taxpayer is required to file even though none of his income is taxable. To determine whether a person should file a return, a tax preparer must check the taxpayer's **Form W-2** and/or **Form(s) 1099.**

Who needs to file?

The numbers change based on COLA (cost of living adjustments), so consider these only as an example:

You need to file if your gross income exceeds the last column in the schedule shown. You need to file if you received over $400 in a 1099Misc with the amount in box 7 the IRS considers you self employed for that.

Note: In the schedule below, dependents are not calculated, and although Exemptions are gone in 2018 tax, but here are used to show the income for filing requirement.

Filing Status	Deduction	Exemptions	Add'l	Add'l	Total
Single	$ 6,400	$ 4,100			$ 10,5 00
Single--over 65	6,400	$ 4,100	$ 1,600		$ 12,100
Married, Filing Separately	$ -	$ 4,100			$ 4,100
Married, Filing Jointly	$ 12,800	$ 8,200			$ 21,000
Married, both over 65 or blind	$ 12,800	$ 8,200	$ 1,300	$ 1,300	$ 23,600
Married, one of the spouses blind or over 65	$ 12,800	$ 8,200	$ 1,600		$ 22,400
Head of Household and a dependent-under 65	$ 9,400	$ 8,200			$ 17,600
Head of Household, and a dependent over 65	$ 9,400	$ 8,200	$ 1,600		$ 19,000

Keep in mind that these rules apply to dependents who are also married, not just simply married taxpayers. For tax purposes, your spouse is never considered your dependent.

Nonresident Aliens and Form 1040NR

Taxpayers who are not citizens or legal residents (green card holders) are generally considered nonresidents for income tax purposes. Legal resident aliens (green card holders) are taxed in the same way as U.S. citizens. "Residency" for tax purposes is not the same as legal residency for green card status. It is an important concept to understand. An individual may still be considered a "U.S. resident" for tax purposes, based on the physical time he or she spends in the United States.

A nonresident can be someone who lives outside the U.S. and simply invests in U.S. property or stocks, and is therefore required to file a tax return in order to correctly report his or her earnings. Each year, thousands of nonresident aliens are also gainfully employed in the United States. Thousands more own rental property or earn interest or dividends from U.S. investments, and are therefore required to file U.S. tax returns.

How to Determine Alien Tax Status:

If the taxpayer is an alien (not a U.S. citizen), she is considered a *nonresident* for tax purposes *unless* she meets one of two tests:

1. **The Green Card Test:** A taxpayer is considered a U.S. resident if she is a lawful permanent resident of the United States (if the taxpayer has a "green card"). Green card holders are taxed just like U.S. citizens, regardless of where they live.

2. **The "Substantial Presence" Test:** The "Substantial Presence" test is based on a calendar year (January 1 – December 31). A taxpayer will also be considered a U.S. resident for tax purposes only if she meets the "substantial presence" test for the calendar year. To meet this test, the taxpayer must be physically present in the United States on at least:

   - 31 days during the current year, and
   - 183 days during the previous three years.

   When counting days of physical presence, count:
   - All the days he was present in the current year, and
   - One-third of the days he was present in the first year before the current year, and

- One-sixth of the days he was present in the second year before the current year

Taxpayers that qualify as U.S. residents (including all U.S. citizens and green card holders) must file a U.S. tax return (unless they are exempt, such as taxpayers who are below the income requirements), and ALL their worldwide income is subject to U.S. tax and must be reported on their U.S. tax return (**Form 1040**, *U.S. Individual Income Tax Return*). If the taxpayer does *not* meet either the Green Card Test or the Substantial Presence Test, then the taxpayer is considered a nonresident for tax purposes.

Note: Nonresident aliens are subject to U.S. income tax only on their U.S. source income.

Section II: ANALYSIS OF ALL TAXPAYER'S INCOME

Chapter III: Taxable Income

1. Wages, salaries, bonuses and commissions
2. Interest income (Schedule B and 1099 INT) and Dividends (1099 DIV)
3. Capital gains (from sale of property or securities, Schedule D). ***Note***: Capital loss is a negative income—which means although it's part of income in 1040; it will reduce your income.
4. Farm income (Schedule F)
5. Business income/Self-employment income (Schedule C)
6. Partnership, estate and S-corporation income (Schedule K-1s, taxpayer's share)
7. Tips and gratuities
8. Breach of contract
9. Awards
10. Back pay
11. Compensation for personal services
12. Director's fees
13. Disability benefits (employer-funded)
14. Discounts
15. Employee awards
16. Employee bonuses
17. Severance pay
18. Unemployment compensation
19. Rewards
20. Annuities
21. Debts forgiven (if the taxpayer received a Form 1099-C, Cancellation of Debt, in relation to their main home, it can be nontaxable (see D-4)
22. Estate and trust income
23. Fees
24. Interest on life insurance dividends
25. IRA distributions
26. Military pay (not exempt from taxation)
27. Military pension
28. Notary fees
29. Pensions

30. Rents (gross rent)
31. Royalties
32. Self-employment
33. Non-employee compensation
34. Social security benefits - portion may be taxable ***Note*: See TaxWise Tab 2 - Income, the page for Railroad Retirement, Civil Service, and Social Security Benefits
35. Supplemental unemployment benefits
36. Taxable scholarships and grants
37. Other Income:

    a. Alimony, (whereas Child Support has always been non-taxable income, Alimony was taxable until 2018)
    b. Gambling winnings
    c. Hobby income
    d. Punitive damage
    e. Railroad retirement—Tier I (portion may be taxable)
    f. Railroad retirement—Tier II
    g. Refund of state taxes
    h. Jury duty fees

Income

Attach Form(s) W-2 here. Also attach Forms W-2G and 1099-R if tax was withheld.

If you did not get a W-2, see instructions.

Enclose, but do not attach, any payment. Also, please use Form 1040-V.

7	Wages, salaries, tips, etc. Attach Form(s) W-2		7	
8a	Taxable interest. Attach Schedule B if required			
b	Tax-exempt interest. Do not include on line 8a . . .	8b		
9a	Ordinary dividends. Attach Schedule B if required		9a	
b	Qualified dividends	9b		
10	Taxable refunds, credits, or offsets of state and local income taxes		10	
11	Alimony received			
12	Business income or (loss). Attach Schedule C or C-EZ		12	
13	Capital gain or (loss). Attach Schedule D if required. If not required, check here ▶ ☐		13	
14	Other gains or (losses). Attach Form 4797		14	
15a	IRA distributions .	15a	b Taxable amount . . .	15b	
16a	Pensions and annuities	16a	b Taxable amount	16b	
17	Rental real estate, royalties, partnerships, S corporations, trusts, etc. Attach Schedule E		17	
18	Farm income or (loss). Attach Schedule F		18	
19	Unemployment compensation		19	
20a	Social security benefits	20a	b Taxable amount . . .	20b	
21	Other income. List type and amount _____		21	
22	Combine the amounts in the far right column for lines 7 through 21. This is your **total income** ▶		22	

(Copy to use as Example FKianFA)

Exhibit 5: This summary income needs as much attention as deductions

Chapter IV: Non-Taxable Income

1. Aid to Families with Dependent Children (AFDC)
2. Child support (whereas alimony is taxable)
3. Damages for physical injury (other than punitive)
4. Death payments
5. Dividends on life insurance
6. Federal Employees' Compensation Act payments
7. Federal income tax refunds
8. Gifts, bequests, and inheritances (remember, gift reporting is the responsibility of the donor)
9. Insurance proceeds
   - Accident
   - Casualty
   - Health
   - Life

   An inheritance is not reported on the income tax return, but a distribution from an inherited pension or annuity is subject to the same tax as the original owner would have had to pay.

10. Interest on tax-free securities
11. Interest on EE/I bonds redeemed for qualified higher education expenses
12. Meals and lodging for the convenience of employer
13. Payments to the beneficiary of a deceased employee
14. Relocation payments or payments in lieu of worker's compensation
15. Rental allowance of clergyman
16. Sickness and injury payments
17. Social security benefits - portion may not be taxable

***Note*: See TaxWise Tab 2 - Income, the page for Railroad Retirement, Civil Service, and Social Security Benefits

18. Supplemental Security Income (SSI)
19. Temporary Assistance for Needy Families (TANF)
20. Veterans' benefits
21. Welfare payments (including TANF) and food stamps
22. Worker's compensation and similar payments

Note: From 2019 going forth, Alimony may not be taxable income

Chapter V: Recognize Earned and Unearned Income

Earned Income Includes what you earned with blood, sweat and tears:

1. Taxable wages, salaries, and tips
2. Union strike benefits
3. Taxable long-term disability benefits received prior to minimum retirement age
4. Net earnings from self-employment
5. Gross income of a statutory employee
6. Household employee income
7. Nontaxable combat pay election
8. Non-Employee compensation
9. The rental value of a home or a housing allowance provided to a minister as part of the minister's pay

Earned Income Excludes what you get because of the old-time work, or what you had to put up in the past, or your parents' legacy.

1. Interest and dividends
2. Social security and railroad retirement benefits
3. Welfare benefits
4. Workfare payments
5. Pensions and annuities
6. Veteran's benefits (including VA rehabilitation payments)
7. Workers' compensation benefits
8. Alimony
9. Child support
10. Nontaxable foster-care payments
11. Unemployment compensation
12. Taxable scholarship or fellowship grant that is not reported on Form W-2
13. Earnings for work performed while an inmate at a penal institution*
14. Salary deferrals (for example, under a 401(k) or 403(b) plan or the Federal Thrift Savings Plan)
15. The value of meals or lodging provided by an employer for the convenience of the employer
16. Disability Insurance payments

17. Excludable dependent care benefits (line 24 of Form 2441)
18. Salary reductions such as under a cafeteria plan
19. Excludable employer-provided educational assistance benefits (may be shown in box 13 of Form W-2)
20. Anything else of value received from someone for services performed, if it is not currently taxable

Gross Income

Gross income means all income you received in the form of money, goods, property, and services that is not exempt from tax, including any income from sources outside the United States or from the sale of your main home (even if you can exclude part or all of it).

Do not include any social security benefits unless either:

a. you are married filing a separate return and you lived with your spouse at any time
b. one-half of your social security benefits plus your other gross income and any tax-exempt interest is more than $25,000 ($32,000 if married filing jointly)

Gross income includes gains, but not losses (reported on Form 8949). Gross income from a business means, for example, the amount on Schedule C, or Schedule F, but in figuring gross income, do not reduce your income by any losses, including any loss on Schedule C, line 7, or Schedule F, line 9.

 Example:
Rachel is 36 years old, single, and her gross income was $20,000. She does not have any children. She must file a tax return and will use the Single filing status since her income was over the non-filers' threshold.

There are special rules for dependents with taxable income, self-employed persons, and nonresident aliens.

Generally, if a dependent child who must file an income tax return cannot file it for any reason, such as age, then the parent (or other legally responsible person) must file it on the child's behalf. If a child cannot sign his or her own tax return, the guardian must sign the child's name followed by the words "By (signature), parent for minor child." See Kiddie Tax later on in this study guide.

Not all income is taxable. There are many types of income that are *reportable*, but not taxable, to the recipient. Even if a taxpayer is not legally required to file a tax return, she should if eligible to receive a refund. Taxpayers should still file tax returns if any of the following are true:

    a. They had income tax withheld from their pay
    b. They made estimated tax payments or had a prior year overpayment
    c. They qualify for the Earned Income Tax Credit (EITC)
    d. They qualify for the child tax credit (which is a refundable credit)

Income that are shown on Schedules:

Schedule B: Interest Income

Interest income is the interest Taxpayers often receive Form 1099-Int.
You use Schedule B if your interest income is more than $1,500

- Interest is reported on Schedule B (IRS checks your reported interest against the bank's)
- If interest earned is shared with someone else, you need to declare all as it appears in the 1099, then:
    - Issue a 1099 to send to nominee (the other shareholder)
    - In schedule B you enter complete amount of 1099, and on line 2 deduct the share you sent to "nominee"
    - Along with 1096 Transmittal of Information Return". 80
- Reporting interests on bond bought.
- OID (original Issue Discount) of bond must be reported as interest (form 1099-OID)

NOTE: Credit Unions and Saving and Bonds counts you as members thus don't' pay 'interest' and usually send your 1099 declaring them as Dividends. Remember, they are Interest income, nonetheless.

Example:
Bond issued at face value of $1,000 and offered at $900.
1. Do you need to declare anything?

2. Using cash basis?
3. Using accrual basis?

Solution:
1. $100 in interest is accrued, so that interest should be declared
2. If cash basis, NO
3. If accrual basis, YES

Interest and Dividends

At the time this publication went to print, screen shots of the new Forms Schedule D (Form 1040), Capital Gains and Losses and new Form 8949, Sales and Other Dispositions of Capital Assets were not available.

You may receive a K-1 from your client. Check line 5 and 6 on the K-1. If you see interest and dividends, these numbers will go on 1040 line 8 and 9 as well.
US savings Bonds: They are taxable interest: Series HH Bonds pays interest twice a year that has to be reflected on interest. (Not taxable for State) they mature in 20 years.
Bonds EE. Interest comes when you redeemed. You can accrue the interest if you want.
Series I. issued in 1998, fixed interest plus inflation rate. Mature 30 years.
See form 8815 to see exclusions and how that can impact your education credit you are claiming

Original Issue Discount. The discount from par value at the time that a bond or other debt instrument is issued. It is the difference between the stated redemption price at maturity and the issue price. Whether you receive the difference or not, it has to be declared as income.

NOTE: On State Bonds: Remember, states do not charge you tax for the state issued bonds, but they charge tax on other states bonds.

Mining Cryptocurrency-Bitcoins

Mining is validating bitcoin transactions by computer. If there's a difference between taxpayers basis and the FMV, then the taxpayer must recognize the gain. The type of currency is immaterial, and as far as tax is concerned income is taxable no matter how it was paid. If the cryptocurrency is used to buy inventory the gain is an ordinary income, and if the currency is used to buy stocks or other capital assets, the excess worth of the currency is capital gain.

With the same token, if an employee receives bitcoin as payroll, it is constitutes wages and are subject to withholdings, and a payment to independent contractor for his/her services is subject to self employment income tax. If a company paid over $600 for a service by bitcoin, the company is required to submit a 1099-Misc. The Fair Market Value (FMV) of the virtual currency is determined on the date of payment in US dollars.

If bitcoins are paid as services provided and even not converted to the US dollar by the recipient, it's still an income to the recipient just the same way as a barter valued when received.

Although the IRS has not yet developed guidelines for exchange of cryptocurrency, any exchange has to be interpreted similar to stock ownership. So one type of cryptocurrency could be considered "LIKE-KIND" exchange with another cryptocurrency, and not other securities for 2017 and earlier. IRS has established that LIKE_KIND exchange beginning 2018 only applies to real properties.

As far as reporting the transactions in cryptocurrency, the same penalties that applies to underreporting of payment is also applied to the taxpayers who pay through cryptocurrency and do not report it properly.
See https://investing.com/currencies/btc-usd-historical-data.

Example:
John purchased $10,000 in bitcoins on June 2nd as investment. He sold them for $160,000 in November. John will declare $150,000 in short-term gain on his schedule D. So if his income was $210,000, he would pay 35% gain on this gain. **The tax on this gain is 35% or $52,500 in taxes on his $150,000 gains.**

What would've been his tax rate if he had waited for a year (assuming the same selling price)?

Solution: His tax would be 15% of this gain: $22,500. $30,000 less. Have we established that patience is a virtue that pays you $30,000 more?

Schedule C - Profit and Loss from Business

A business activity is an activity for generating profit. If a business makes a profit in at least three of the last five tax years, including the current year (or at least two of the last seven years for activities that consist primarily of breeding, showing, training or racing horses) it may considered a business activity (See Business Vs. Hobby below).

A Self Employed operating a Sole Proprietor operating under his/her own Social Security number of a fictitious name is not considered Employee and does not receive a payroll check.

This Self Employed individual is not receiving wages from anyone, but fees for providing services or sales of product, etc. and is responsible for his/her own taxes. If an activity is not for profit, losses from that activity may not be used to offset other income. An activity produces a loss when related expenses exceed income. The limit on not-for-profit losses applies to individuals, partnerships, estates, trusts, and S corporations. It does not apply to corporations other than S corporations.

Gig Economy:

Americanism is all about the dream of freedom, but form the last century until now, freedom is sacrificed for security. People wanted job security, insurance, retirement and all the good things the employment could provide even-though they did not offer fair wages. People still wanted the job security until they found out that no job was secure. Many started their own business as self employed and discovered freedom in having flexible schedule or no schedule at all (such as Airbnb and Uber).

A tremendous social upheaval is in progress and not many are aware of how gig economy will change the whole fabric of Midwestern States particularly those who don't engage in using technological services such as the Internet as gig economy is mostly available in big cities.

Let see how we can build a wall to stop computers and robots from taking the American jobs. But then again, I think that was has already built and people who constantly need supervision, are being deported out of the companies every day. No matter what kind of Gig Economy you are engaged in, the tax laws is applicable to you, and remember, cash receipts are also income.

Use Schedule C (Form 1040) to report income or loss from a business you operated or a profession you practiced as a sole proprietor. An activity qualifies as a business if your primary purpose for engaging in the activity is for income or profit and you are involved in the activity with continuity and regularity. For example, a sporadic activity or a hobby does not qualify as a business. A taxpayer can use Schedule C-EZ if business expenses are $5,000 or less but if the self employed Taxpayer had a loss from his business or engaged in selling inventory, he/she cannot use Schedule C-EZ

❖ Also Sole Member LLCs with no employees will reflect their income and loss in Schedule C.

❖ The Sole Proprietors who usually use their Social Security as their Identifying number need to show this number in every business inquiries, therefore they may put themselves at risk. It's recommended they apply for EIN to deal with outside vendors and pay taxes using the EIN.

Business Income and Expenses
All income received during the course of business is the business income even though they may not be in cash.

Gross Receipts are all income combined for conducting business that may include

- Sales
- Services
- What cash inflow is not considered income
- Barter
- Consignments
- Commissions, prizes, gifts, etc.

- Interest and dividends income and imputed interest (unpaid, but accrued—particularly on bonds)
- Recovery of charge offs

Use the Schedule C to report (a) wages and expenses you had as a statutory employee, (b) income and deductions of certain qualified joint ventures, and (c) certain income shown on Form 1099-MISC, Miscellaneous Income.

Note that all businesses are required to send you a 1099 miscellaneous if you have provided services exceeding $600. Likewise, you will notice bellow that you are required to issue 1099 Miscellaneous for anyone who performed services for you to justify the expenses. Although taxpayers who earn less than $10,000 of income are not required to file for taxes, the self- employed individual who receives a 1099 for even $400 is required to file a tax return.

Example. Tom is an insurance agent and small business consultant. He takes one of his clients golfing and out to lunch to give guidance on a business transaction and sell an insurance policy.

Write-off? Nope. Because the activity occurred in 2018, Tom gets no deduction and arguably the meal isn't a write-off either.

First, all small businesses and entrepreneurs are affected; no one is exempt from this provision in the new tax law. Sole-proprietors, S-Corporations, LLCs and C-Corporations – all beware.

Prior law

So long as an expense was directly related to (or, in some cases, even associated with), the active conduct of a trade or business, you were allowed a deduction for an activity generally considered to be entertainment, amusement, or recreation. The limit was up to 50% of the expense, but it was still *something* and oftentimes worth the expense to do some business while 'entertaining'.

New Law

No deductions for entertainment. Period. See what is considered as entertainment:

- Any activity generally considered to be entertainment, amusement or recreation

- Membership dues to any club organized for recreation or social purposes

- A facility, or portion thereof, used in connection with the above items

  That means no more deduction for a round of golf, theater tickets, spa visit, sports tickets, skybox, fishing, hunting, show tickets, etc... This is a big deal!!

  Here are the major parts to be completed. It's granted that all expense items have to include a back-up and also show they are directly related to business:

Part I. Income

All business Related Income(and if incurred provided discounts, returns, etc. deduct them here to come up with net sale)

NOTE: Sales of the company Assets, although they bring cash to the bank, are not considered Income. They may result in Capital Gain and Capital Loss, as we'll discuss in Schedule D.

Part II. Expenses:

These are all Business related expenses (expenses incurred to generate income.)

a. Use only expenses allowed in Part II. Make sure all expenses are directly related to business activity and aimed at producing income.

b. If you are using your home, then use part 30 and on

c. Record keeping is the key to back-up your expenses. If you lost a receipt for instance, the IRS may not accept the expense, or even your PC if you cannot show proof of purchase.

d. Remember, as a self-employed, you will not have wages and are not issuing yourself a W-2, but you can employ an pay wages and at the end of the year, you will issue W-2 so that your employees can file their taxes with the evidence of income. (needless to say, you have back up to show you have employee expenses.

e. Once you issued the W-2s at the end of the year, you also are required to issue W-3 to show the total W-2s you have issued.

Also see the TCJA rules for elimination of some business expenses.

2. **Part III. Cost of Goods Sold**

Details (remember, this is only for inventory based businesses—not for service industry.) An example of other organizations to use Cost of Goods Sold are some service industry such as those who need outside contractors (such as construction companies will show all material and labor that was used to complete a project by outside contractors. A form need to be completed to show Beginning Inventory, plus purchases, labor, and overhead, minus ending inventory. Check out **Business Tax Made Easy** by the same author for more explanation of CGS with some examples.

3. **Part IV. Information on Vehicle** used by company. Here again, recordkeeping for business miles have to be kept as an excel log or digital mile tracker to show all business miles are indeed to produce income. I have noticed that some clients put the same numbers in Form 2106 their personal deduction as well as on schedule C. Simple human error, you say? Not when the IRS gets the short end of the stick all the time.

Mileage Rate in 2018
- ➤ The standard mileage rate for transportation or travel expenses is 54.5 cents per mile for all miles of business use.
- ➤ The standard mileage rate is 14 cents per mile for use of an automobile in rendering gratuitous services to a charitable organization under.
- ➤ The standard mileage rate is 18 cents per mile for use of an automobile (1) for medical care and for moving to a new job (up from 17 cents in 2017)

Based on Notice 2018-03 of the IRS, For automobiles a taxpayer uses for business purposes, the portion of the business standard mileage rate treated as depreciation is 22 cents per mile for 2014, 24 cents per mile for 2015, 24 cents per mile for 2016, 25 cents per mile for 2017, and 25 cents per mile for 2018.

For purposes of computing the allowance, the standard automobile cost may not exceed $27,300 for automobiles (excluding trucks and vans) or $31,000 for trucks and vans

See https://www.irs.gov/pub/irs-drop/n-18-03.pdf for more details

Definition of Income & Expenses

In short,

Business Income relates proceeds due to a business activity:

The income generated as a result of conducting business such as sales or services. Be aware that in a bank statement, not all cash that comes into the business is income and not all monies, checks, wire, or withdrawals are considered expenses (they could be the premise of Cash Flow instead of Income Statement).

Also remember what the IRS calls Income, accountants call it Revenues or Fees, or other terms depending on the industry.

Before you complete your income, you also need to deduct the returns and discounts (they are not expenses).

For instance sale of inventory is Income but sales of Furniture or equipment that was supposed to be used in your office is not an Income (those sales only impact your capital gain or loss)

Expenses:

All items classified as business expense is related to items purchase to use to generate profit. Therefore if a business purchased a computer, or a printer to perform services, it can expense out these items or account them as assets. Whichever chosen, there must be a company note or minute to describe what items will be expenses and what items are assets.

I used to work for a company that considered anything under $1,000 as expense (such as chairs or printers). There must be a system in place to define this decision and the company has to stay consistence unlike the old Enron that one year classified an item as expenses to pay less taxes, and put them as assets in another year, to satisfy the shareholders with higher return.

The next thing to consider is Expenses have to be related to generating income. So if you purchased computer for office, it could be expense, but not the one you purchased to use for personal work.

Section 199-A

(See Cornell Law School website for more information)

The TCJA establishes a 20 percent deduction of qualified business income from certain pass-through businesses. Specific service industries, such as health, law, and professional services, are excluded. However, joint filers with income below $315,000(MFJ) and other filers with income below $157,500 can claim the deduction fully on income from service industries. This provision would expire December 31, 2025.

If the taxable income increased from the above thresholds, then the QBI amount would be greater of:

- [ ] 50% of wages from the qualified trade or business or
- [ ] 25% of wages plus 2.5% of the unadjusted basis of qualified property from the qualified trade or business.

For those taxpayers between $157,500-207,500 ($305,000-415,000 MFJ) the limitation is phased out.

The deduction does not apply to Specified Service Trade or Business (SSTB) otherwise known as Personal Business Corporations. Which is to say, the following businesses cannot rake the 20% deductions as described if their income exceeds the thresholds mentioned above:

Any trade or business involving the performance of services in the fields of health, law, engineering, architecture, accounting, actuarial science, performing arts, consulting, athletics, financial services, brokerage services, or any trade or business where the principal asset of such trade or business is the reputation or skill of 1 or more of its employees.

The shareholders will deduct 20% of the business income against itself, which will be claimed as a below-the-line (but not itemized) deduction for tax purposes, effectively making them taxed on only 80 cents of each dollar they earn. This reduces the top marginal tax rate on pass-through business entities from a new top tax rate of 37%, down to a reduced rate of 37% x 80% = 29.6%. However, the new QBI rules do not permit the deduction for high-income "Professional Service Companies or Specified Service (including lawyers, accountants, doctors, consultants, and financial advisors).

The easiest way to recognize the benefit is to use Section 199A (as described in the IRS website and Cornell Law as referenced above). In short a taxpayer shows a 20% deduction of the pass-thru income within his (her) 1040. This 80% income from the pass-thru is added to wages or other income in the taxpayer's 1040 to figure the gross income.

Just note that 20% credit is helpful for those who do make better profit. If the business is losing money, there's no benefit from this credit. if an entrepreneur is not making income, there's no benefit in the 20% credit.

Example: Ruth and Jim (MFJ) have a collective income of $190,000. Jim's W2 shows $90,000 and Ruth's clothing store shows $100,000 income. What is their taxable income?

Solution: In 2018, the couple will be eligible for a $24,000 standard deduction, reducing their income to $166,000. In addition, they will receive a $20,000 QBI credit for Ruth's business income, further reducing their income to $146,000.

(See more on Section 199-A used in this Study Guide in Trump/GOP Tax Cuts-F. Kian 2018)

Is it a Hobby or is it a Business?

In general, taxpayers may deduct ordinary and necessary expenses for conducting a trade or business or for the production of income. Trade or business activities and activities engaged in for the production of income are activities engaged in for profit. The most important distinction between a business activity and a hobby is recordkeeping.

Internal Revenue Code Section 183 (Activities Not Engaged in for Profit) limits deductions that can be claimed when an activity is not engaged in for profit. IRC 183 is sometimes referred to as the "hobby loss rule."

The following factors, although not all inclusive, may help you to determine whether your activity is an activity engaged in for profit or a hobby:

- Does the time and effort put into the activity indicate an intention to make a profit?
- Do you depend on income from the activity?
- If there are losses, are they due to circumstances beyond your control or did they occur in the start-up phase of the business?
- Have you changed methods of operation to improve profitability?
- Do you have the knowledge needed to carry on the activity as a successful business?
- Have you made a profit in similar activities in the past?
- Does the activity make a profit in some years?
- Do you expect to make a profit in the future from the appreciation of assets used in the activity?

What are the allowable hobby deductions under IRC 183?

If your activity is not carried on for profit, allowable deductions cannot exceed the gross receipts for the activity.

Deductions for hobby activities are claimed as itemized deductions on Schedule A, Form 1040. These deductions must be taken in the following order and only to the extent stated in each of three categories:

- Deductions that a taxpayer may claim for certain personal expenses, such as home mortgage interest and taxes, may be taken in full.
- Deductions that don't result in an adjustment to the basis of property, such as advertising, insurance premiums and wages, may be taken next, to the extent gross income for the activity is more than the deductions from the first category.
- Deductions that reduce the basis of property, such as depreciation and amortization, are taken last, but only to the extent gross income for the activity is more than the deductions taken in the first two categories.

Home Office Expensing

Generally, the IRS has offered two alternative ways to calculate your home office deductions:

- **Regular system** which is based on the actual cost incurred for home office; for instance, if you use a whole room or part of a room for conducting your business, you need to figure out the percentage of your home devoted to your business activities as well as the percentage of time you spent in there. As a rule, Bedroom is not a good place to be assigned as a home office, unless…. Then again, no!

- **Simplified Version** (that went into effect in 2014) to use some type of a standard deduction—just like your standard mileage rates. The highlight of Simplified version are as follows:
  - Standard deduction of $5 per square foot of home used for business (maximum 300 square feet).
  - Allowable home-related itemized deductions claimed in full on Schedule A. (For example: Mortgage interest, real estate taxes).
  - No home depreciation deduction or later recapture of depreciation for the years the simplified option is used.

To deduct home office cost, use Form 8829. These conditions must be met:

1- Your principal place of business—exclusively.

2. A place to meet or deal with clients

3- A separate structure (greenhouse) that is used in connection with your business

File only with Schedule C (Form 1040). Use a separate Form 8829 for each home you used for business during the year.

If you own your home and use 20% for business, what are the portions of the **Indirect Expense** you can deduct as business expense? Can you deduct the landscaping or lawn maintenance cost?

If you rent and then allocate 20% of your home to business and your rent is $1,500 a month, what is your business rent? Do you have other deductions?

EXAMPLE:

An individual uses 50% of her house as a daycare. 12 hours a day, five days a week, 50 weeks per year. (Her family uses of the basement during off hours)

1. What is her ratio of business to personal use?
2. How much indirect expenses can be allocated for daycare?
3. If the monthly indirect expenses total $2,000 for the house, how much can be deducted as home office expense?

SOLUTION:

- 12x 5 x 50= 3,000 hours a year
- 3,000/8,760=34.25% of total hours.

    Since 50% of her home was used for business thus 34.25 x 50%= 17.13% of all indirect expenses can be claimed as business expense.

    17.3 x 2,000= $346 per month

Recordkeeping requirements

What distinguishes a business from a hobby is recordkeeping. The IRS doesn't care what program you use, but how you can backup certain expenses. Use what makes your records clearly and to show how you incurred an expense to increase the sales.

Four special statements can help a business show proper record keeping.

- Profit and Loss from business is the main statement. Schedule C is a good place to help one organize the various expenses and perhaps the most important statement to produce schedule C for small business.
- Balance Sheet can help a business owner to reflect assets and show how they decided to depreciate assets and amortize liabilities.
- Bank Reconciliation and—Bank statements can help business owner to show all moneys coming into the business and leaving the bank.
- Inventory tracking system or inventory statement to show the beginning inventory and ending inventory as well as purchases can help business to figure out Cost of Goods Sold.

For small business, it's important to keep a good log of business mile every year and basically for tracking every business activities to show the mileage had a business impact. Remember: Any bills paid by the business for business purposes is used. So if your condo manager sent you a bill unrelated to your business, it does not need to be recorded in business books.

Schedule D Capital Gains and Losses

Schedule D is to show gain from Capital Assets (home, Office, furniture, equipment etc.) It also allows for information return matching, including both new Forms **1099B** showing basis and securities bought before 2016 that don't show basis.   If some of the stocks you own pay dividends, or a mutual fund you invest in made a capital gains distribution to you during the year, you'll receive a 1099-DIV form.

If you sold a covered security in 2017, your broker will send you a Form 1099-DIV(or substitute statement) that shows your basis Both the short and long sections of Schedule D bring in amounts from new Form 8949 (which replaces Schedule D-1) separating three types of transactions. Individual transactions will no longer be listed on Schedule D.

To calculate the net Capital Gain (loss), taxpayer needs to net out the Short terms gain from short term losses and then Long Term Gains netted against the long term losses. Finally the net of short term is netted out against the long term gain (or loss).

Form 8949 - Sales and Other Dispositions of Capital Assets

Form 8949 will contain all capital gain and loss transactions. None will be reported directly on Schedule D. The subtotals from Form 8949 will be carried over to Schedule D (Form 1040), where gain or loss will be calculated in aggregate. Short and long-term transactions are listed by the following categories:

- Transactions reported on Form 1099-B that show basis in box 3
- Transactions reported on Form 1099-B that do not show basis in box 3
- Transactions not reported on Form 1099-B

Sales of Personal Residence:

If you own your home for at least 5 years and live in there for 2 years prior to selling the house, then up to 250,000 of your gain is tax free ($500,000 for MFJ).

Sales of Inheritance:

If a taxpayer inherited any assets there are two ways to establish the capital impact:

A. If the owner has established basis for the asset, that will be the basis for the inheritance.

B. If the owner has not established a legitimate basis for the assets, then the Fair Market Value (FMV)at the time of gift (or inheritance) as it's appraised by a professional will be the basis to calculate Capital Gain or Capital loss when the asset is sold.

Note: Fair Market value is the price at which a property would change hands between buyers and sellers in an open and free market.

Reporting Property Sales

Long term Capital Gains (Schedule D Part II) are generally taxed at lower rates than ordinary income.

- ☐ Zero tax on eligible long term capital gains (Part I of Schedule D) for taxpayers with a top bracket for 10% or 15%
- ☐ Separate short term gain (assets held for less than a year) from long term gain
- ☐ Loss on sale to relatives is disallowed

Examples of capital assets - stocks, bonds, land, art, gems, stamps, personal residence, car, jewelry, and other long term investments. You can deduct up to $3, 000 of capital loss (jointly) reported on Schedule D (if total loss is more than $3,000 carry it forward). Assets for personal use are not deductible.

Note: If married, filing jointly, the gain of one spouse may offset loss of the other.

Example:
If you bought a property for $5,000 and exchanged it later for a $3,000 property, no loss is reported (if it's sold for $3,000, then it is a capital loss. If it is sold for $12,000, then it is a capital gain of $7,000) for **Like** properties.
If **Unlike** (not same category), you need to recognize the profit or loss.

Transfers between spouses are tax free—unless one is a nonresident alien. Sales of your residence can also provide for tax free capital gain if you live there 2 out of five years prior to sales.

See if you can practice on these 3 examples:

1. What happens if you bought a property for $5,000 and exchanged it later for a $5,000 property?

2. You bought a property for $5,000 and sold it for 50,000?

3. If you bought a property for $5,000 and exchanged it later for $3,000 worth of equipment?

Capital Gain (Loss) Terms you will encounter

☐ **Cost basis:** Original purchase cost, plus commissions or fees paid at time of purchase

☐ **Holding period:** Time between the date of purchase and date of sale

☐ **Sales price:** Proceeds of sale of asset, gross or net, reported on Form 1099-B

If there is no Form 1099-B, taxpayer must provide this information

Where to report: Schedule D and Form 8949

Holding Period:
Short-term holding period: 1 year or less (Taxed at regular income tax rates)
Long-term holding period: More than 1 year (Taxed at a lower rate than short-term)

Mutual fund shares are generally acquired at various times, in various quantities, and at various prices; figuring the basis can be difficult. Refer to Pub 550 for information on how to report the sale or exchange of mutual fund shares

Blocks of stock may have differing holding periods and bases. Unless specified at the time of sale, blocks/shares are sold using FIFO method (first in, first out)

Gain must be reported when

☐ Amount is greater than the allowed exclusion.

☐ Home is *not* the taxpayer's main home
☐ If taxpayer received Form 1099-S for their gain or loss on the sale of a main home, it must be reported on Form 8949 and Schedule D

Taxpayers may be able to exclude from taxable income the gain from sale of a main home. Up to a maximum of $250,000 ($500,0000 for Married Filing Jointly)

You need to confirm the home sold was the taxpayer's main home, and the taxpayer meets the ownership and use tests.

Example:

Celina Gomez lives with her parents in the same house since 2015. She buys the house from her parents last , and sells it around June this year at a gain for $220,000. Can she qualify for tax on gain?

Solution: No. Although Celina (is famous and) had lived there for 10 years, but she did not own the house. She does not meet the USE Test

Example: Johnny D. Epp bought a house in Jan 2009 and lived there until Oct. 1st. 2010. He took a year off to visit the Caribbean's, and when he came back, he didn't like the house anymore and sold it.

• Does he meet the two year use test?

• How could he have avoided tax on gain?

Solution

Johnny D. Epp does not meet the two year use test, because his leave was not a short, temporary absent. He can avoid tax on gains if he can show
- Job change
- Poor health,
- Unforeseen circumstances
- He had gone there for a job (movie)

Example:

You and your spouse lived in the same house for 10 years, and then sold it last year for $450,000. How much is taxable?

Solution

No tax on this gain, since you meet the ownership and use test.

Example:

A husband and wife live in a house for 3 years, Unfortunately the wife died in March of last year. In November of that same year the poor husband marries and lives with his high-school sweetheart and everything was great for a year—when...

- ☐ The new wife notices ghosts all over the place, so they decide to sell the haunted house and move.
- ☐ The gain is $350, 000 on their joint return. Do they report a gain?

Solution

He can only qualify for $250,000 because your new wife lived there less than 9 months. The other 100,000 is taxable.

Additional Interest, NAEOB, and State Adjustment Entries

NAEOB column - Enter:

N – Nominee interest - interest transferred to another person
A – Accrued interest - interest paid to seller at time of purchase
E – Federal tax exempt interest
O – OID – generally not used since most interest reported on Form 1099-OID is fully taxable and should be entered as ordinary interest
B – Amortized bond premium - see IRS Publication 1212 for more details

- ☐ Interest on in-state municipal bonds is NOT taxable on the federal and state returns (second line in screen shot above)
- ☐ Interest on U.S. savings bonds is taxable on the federal return but is NOT taxable on the state return (third line in screen shot above)
- ☐ Interest on out-of-state municipal bonds is NOT taxable on the federal return BUT is taxable on the state return (fourth line in screen shot above)

Schedule E: Rental Income & Expenses, Royalties, and Activities in Partnership, LLC and S Corp:

- Rent you receive
- Insurance proceeds for casualty on rental properties
- Tenant's payment for improvements
- Other bartered benefits in lieu of rent

Rental Deductions

1. Real estate taxes
2. Construction period interest and taxes
3. Depreciation of rental buildings -When you moved out and a renter moved in.
4. Depreciation of furniture and fixtures
5. Management expenses - Commission paid to collect
6. Premiums for fire, liabilities (amortize as accruals)
7. Cost of canceling lease

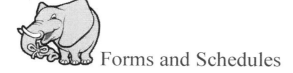 Forms and Schedules

Use **Schedule E to** report Rental Income. If it's a business, then report on **Schedule C.**

- A profit motive is presumed when you can show a profit in 3 out of 5 years engaged in rental activity.
- If you incurred depreciation, taxes, and interest expenses regarding to property income, and never receive the income you expected, your loss is disallowed.
- Rental Activities are Passive income unless you are a Rental Professional or rentals are considered business activities
- If you have a property which is managed by a professional, you cannot deduct losses, even if you spend 300 hours with bookkeeping and budgeting. The activity is passive. Someone else was managing it.
- You can claim loss of $25,000 if you are actively involved in rental activities.
- To qualify, first deduct expenses from losses, then all passive incomes to come up with a loss

Passive-Active Income

- Rental activities are passive income unless you are a rental professional or rentals are considered business activities.
- If you have a property which is managed by a professional, you cannot deduct losses, even if you spend 300 hours with bookkeeping and budgeting. The activity is passive. Someone else was managing it.
- You can claim loss of $25,000 if you are actively involved in rental activities.
- To qualify, first deduct expenses from income, then from all passive incomes to come up with a loss

Example:
Ross in 2010 has $90,000 salary, $15,000 income from a limited partnership, and $26,000 loss from rental where he is actively involved. There is no other income. What is Jim's maximum loss?

Solution:
If he files jointly, he can declare a $25,000 loss.
If he is single, he can declare a $12,500 loss.

***Note*: The maximum $25,000 ($12,500 if filing separately) is reduced by 50% if MAGI is over $100,000 ($50,000 filing separately).

Active Income (for Real Estate Professionals)

Have 10% or more interest in property

More than 750 hours of your services is in real property business.

More than 50% of your business income is from real property business in which you materially participate:

- Real property development
- Redevelopment
- Construction, acquisition, rental operation, management, leasing, brokerage (Real estate financing is not included; personal service as an employee is not treated as professional)
- You set rental terms for your agent to follow and you have the final approval of any rental arrangement or repair authorization

Distinguish Repair from Improvement

Repair:
- Painting, fixing gutters, floors, leaks, plastering, and replacing windows if broken
- Repair is an expense that can be deducted in the year it is paid

Improvement:
- New windows, new plumbing, putting up a fence, new wiring, paving driveways
- Improvements are an asset, the cost of which can be depreciated in years

Only rented sections of a property qualify for deductions.

 Example:

1-You own a 3 story building and two floors are rented. You can only deduct the expenses of those.

2- You have your home office. That segment that's your office is the only segment you can claim for deductions.

3- In 2019 you bought a property for $150,000 and the land is $30,000. You moved out of the house in March and advertised it for rent on April 1. In June, the first tenant moved in.
1. From what month do you start depreciating?
2. How much is the amount you would consider depreciable?

Solution:
1. As of April 1
2. The base of depreciation is $120,000 (but the amount is not depreciated for the whole year but according to the IRS table form April 1)

See depreciation table: 2.576% on the first year

Generally, cash or the fair market value of property you receive for the use of real estate or personal property is taxable to you as rental income. You can generally deduct expenses of renting property from your rental income. Income and expenses related to real estate rentals are usually reported on Form 1040, Schedule E. If you provide substantial services that are primarily for your tenant's convenience, you report your income and expenses on Form 1040, Schedule C. Income and expenses related to personal property rentals are reported on Form 1040.

Most individuals operate on a cash basis, which means they count their rental income as income when it is actually or constructively received, and deduct their expenses as they are paid.

Typical Rental Incomes:

- Amounts paid to cancel a lease
- Advance rent
- Expenses paid by a tenant

**** *Special Note*: A Security deposit is generally not an income!

Typical Rental Expenses:

- Depreciation (use Form 4562)
- Repairs
- Operating Expenses
- Uncollected rents

Personal Use of Rental Property

- Rental if you used less than 14 days or 10% of the time a year
- Say, you stayed in the property for 20 days in the rentable time and rented it for 220 days of total 250 days.
- 10% of 250 days is 25 days. Since you stayed less than 25 days, you can depreciate it for the full year. This is a rental property.

Example:

You rented out your condo in Florida at a fair market rental of 260 days (this is considered the total possible renting days). You also stayed in this property 27 days (which is inclusive of the 260 days)

1. What is your property considered? Rental or residential?
2. Where does your mortgage interest go?
3. Imagine you rented it for 130 days and you stayed there for 13 days. What's the status of property?

Solution:

1. Residence: 260 days x 10% = 26 days. You stayed 27 days which is more than 10% of the rental, thus it is residential.
2. Since it is residential, the deduction goes on schedule A. If it were rental it would go on Schedule E.
3. The stay is 10% (130 days x 10% = 13 days). Therefore, it's a rental property.

Example:
You rented your condo for 60 days (for $2,000 income) and lived in it yourself for 60 days.

1.   What is the total use of this condo?

Your yearly tax for this property is $800. Interest on the mortgage is $1,800, maintenance is $1,200, and depreciation for the year is $1,500.

2.   How much is your income from this rental property?

3.   How if you had not lived there at all and you rented it for all the 120 days for $4,000?

Solution:

Rental Income	$2,000
Less	
Taxes (50% of $800)	$400
Interest (50% of $1,800)	$900
Maintenance (50% of $1,200)	$600
Total	$100

Depreciation (50% of $1,500) $750, but only $100 is the maximum we can deduct because you lived there. Thus, deductions cannot exceed income.

Royalties

Royalties are also reported on Schedule E. Some examples of royalties:
- Licensing fees received for use of patented article
- Renting fees from copyrighted brands
- Authors and artists advance (if not loan)

Expenses allowed:
- Cost of production of creative properties
- Models, stationeries, supplies, travel, drawings, fees, counsel, government charges, etc.

Amortize the cost over the life of patent (usually 15 years). If you bought a patent, amortize the cost of acquiring it for the remaining life of the patent

Activities in S and LLC and in Real Estate

- You may combine your interest in rental held by partnership or S corporations as a single interest in rental real estate.
- You must show Active participation in the business to avoid passive loss restriction
- You may be able to combine activities in several ventures. (grouping activities)
- To materially participate, one needs to work 500 hours a year in some business (it may be 100 hours in other businesses—depending to participation of other partners).

Material Participation

- Work by you or your spouse.
- 50% of your business must be performed in the real property (in excess of 750 hours). Your spouse participation is just like yours even if spouse does not have any share in business.
- Review and study of financial statements and analysis that is unrelated to day to day management is not considered material participation.

At Risk Ventures

1. Films and video production
2. Exploring for Oil and gas properties
3. Exploring for geothermal deposits
4. Farming and cultivation (not forestry)
5. Only your actual tax investment is at risk. You won't have any personal liability for excess losses. (use form 6198 at risk form)

> Risk depends on ventures you materially participate. I.e. if you participate $1,000 in a venture and sign for $8,000 non-recourse, and then the share of loss is $1,900. Your loss is only to the extent you participated: $1,000.

Some Other Types of Notable Income:

Social Security Benefits

Social Security payments shows up in SSA-1099 at the end of the year. The special tax base for determining whether a taxpayer's benefits are subject to tax equals one-half of Social Security benefits, plus all other income, including tax-exempt income. The dollar thresholds below are not indexed to inflation.

Filing Status	Tax Base	% of Benefits Taxed
Single or Head of Household	$25,000 - $34,000 Over 34,000	50% 85%
MFJ	$32,000 - $44,000 Over $44,000	50% 85%

Tax Formula: Here's a quick way to find out if a taxpayer must pay taxes on their Social Security benefits:

First get total of all **Provisional Income**: (Add one-half of the Social Security income to all other income, including tax-exempt interest).

Then compare that amount to the **base amount** for their filing status. If the total is more than the base amount, some of their benefits may be taxable.

Base Amounts. The three base amounts are:

☐ $25,000 – if taxpayers are single, head of household, qualifying widow or widower with a dependent child or married filing separately and lived apart from their spouse for all of the year.

☐ $32,000 – if they are married filing jointly

☐ $0 – if they are married filing separately and lived with their spouse at any time during the year

Example

Jim Jenkster is single. He earned $19,500 for the year and received $2,000 of interest income and $1,500 from gambling winnings. He also receives $10,000 in Social Security income. ($19,500 + $2,000 + $1,500 + $5,000 = $28,000)

Solution:

Jim's provisional income will come to $28,000. He therefore may have to pay taxes on up to 50% of his Social Security. (28,000-25,000)=3,000, thus $1,500 (50% of excess) is taxable.

On a related note on Social Security: In 2017, payroll taxes are collected on income earned up to $127,200, but in 2018, they'll be collected on income up to $128,700 – (See more at ssa.gov),

Other Income: Insurance Policy

Life insurance proceeds are tax free but interest earned from installments are taxed.

Example:
Mark purchases an insurance policy and pays about 40,000 premium. When he dies, Rachel collects the insurance precede for 200,000. How much is her taxable income?

Answer: Zero.

Transfer for Value rule
If life insurance is transferred for valuable consideration, then only that valuable consideration is tax free.

Adam pays a premium of 4000 for an insurance policy. He transfers it to Carol (not his wife), for a valuable consideration of 7,000. When Carol receives the 10,000. Only 7,000 is not taxable. If carol was a partner or a shareholder, then all 10,000 would be tax free.

Example:
Jim and John are partners and have a partner agreement that allows either partner to purchase the interest of the deceased partner. Rick and Sam have insurance policy, each for $50,000. They can exchange their policies—like exchange with no taxable gain, and upon death of one, the other collect the tax free insurance proceed and then buy the interest of the partner.

Employer's after tax cost to provide insurance:
If an employee (in a 28% tax bracket) pays for his own insurance, $3000 a year, he may benefit to take a $3,000 reduction in salary and let the company pay the $3000 for insurance.

Example:

Salary received by Employee:	$3000
Less: Taxes	- 840
Cash available to employee to buy insurance:	2,160

To pay for $3,000 insurance, Employee needs to find $840 more to pay.

Other Income: Gambling Winning and Losses

For casual gamblers, a day's winning is offset by that day's betting expenses. Only professional gamblers (who have developed certain system) can use the whole year of betting expenses from the year's gambling income.

***Special Note: Use of Prior Years' Returns for Comparison* - Review prior year's tax returns for compliance, accuracy, and completeness.

Section III:

GETTING TO AGI

The main difference between deductions and credits is that deductions reduce the amount of income that is taxed (and is therefore calculated before tax is determined) while credits reduce the amount of tax itself.

Note: It is generally better to use credits to reduce tax liability than deductions since credits reduce your tax dollar for dollar, whereas deductions reduce the amount of taxable income. You will see this in examples following right after the study topics.

Adjusted Gross Income	23	Educator expenses	23			
	24	Certain business expenses of reservists, performing artists, and fee-basis government officials. Attach Form 2106 or 2106-EZ	24			
	25	Health savings account deduction. Attach Form 8889 .	25			
	26	Moving expenses. Attach Form 3903	26			
	27	Deductible part of self-employment tax. Attach Schedule SE .	27			Copy to Use as an Example for KianFA Study Guide
	28	Self-employed SEP, SIMPLE, and qualified plans . .	28			
	29	Self-employed health insurance deduction	29			
	30	Penalty on early withdrawal of savings	30			
	31a	Alimony paid b Recipient's SSN ▶	31a			
	32	IRA deduction	32			
	33	Student loan interest deduction	33			
	34	Tuition and fees. Attach Form 8917	34			
	35	Domestic production activities deduction. Attach Form 8903	35			
	36	Add lines 23 through 35		36		
	37	Subtract line 36 from line 22. This is your **adjusted gross income** . . . . . ▶		37		

For Disclosure, Privacy Act, and Paperwork Reduction Act Notice, see separate instructions.   Cat. No. 11320B   Form **1040** (20'

Exhibit 6: Use deductions to reduce your taxable income.

These amounts reduce your Adjusted Gross Income (AGI):

- Educator expense
- Certain business Expenses of reservists, performing artists and fee-basis government officials. (Form 2106)
- Health saving account deductions (Form 8889)
- Moving expense (form 3903)
- Deductible part of self-employment tax.(Schedule SE)

- Self-Employed SEP, SIMPLE, and qualified plans contribution
- Health insurance premium for self-employed
- Penalty on early withdrawal of savings
- Alimony you paid (before 2017 you need to get the social security of the recipient).
- IRA deduction (your contribution during the year)
- Student loan interest deduction (more helpful if AGI is less than $75,000)
- Tuition and fees (form 8917)
- Domestic production activities Deduction (very useful for engineers, architects, real estate professional up to 9% of income),
- Other deductible expenses to help you acquire income (attorney fees, jury duty payment you gave back, rent and royalty expense, 50% of self-employment tax liabilities)

After you subtracted all these deductions, then you will have your AGI. This is perhaps the most important number in all your calculation because everything else is based on this.

Chapter VI Adjustments: Above the Line Deductions

Educator Expenses

- Up to $250 of out of pocket for computer equipment, software, etc. if you teach 900 hours a year
- Over $250 can be considered miscellaneous expenses
- Up to $4,000 of college tuition if your MAGI does not exceed $65,000 (single) and $2,000 if above $65,000

Certain Business Expenses of Reservists, Performing Artists and Fee-Basis Government Officials

Performing arts-related expenses, storytellers, musician, as well as fee basis state officials

HSA Eligibility

Mind you, most businesses healthcare deduction have come under scrutiny from 2018 on, but if your organization provides any HAS, Archer or Flexibly Spending Arrangements you still can use it. The taxpayers in High Deductible Health Plan (HDHP) can contribute minimum $1,350 and maximum of 6,650 out of pocket as pre tax deferral. For family plans these numbers are doubled (for age 55 and over, $1,000 additional is accepted. To qualify an individual must meet **ALL** of the following requirements:

- Be covered under a high deductible health plan (HDHP) on the first day of any month of the year.
- Have no other health coverage except for allowable "other health coverage." (Publication 969, "Other health coverage")
- Not be claimed as a dependent on someone else's tax return. (Publication 969, "Qualifying for an HSA")
- Not be covered by Medicare (but the individual can be HSA eligible for the months before being covered by Medicare)

***Note*: If the taxpayer does not qualify, but contributions have been made to an HSA, the taxpayer should be referred to a professional tax preparer.

Moving and Travel Expenses

Travel Expense

If you incurred out of pocket expenses for traveling to clients or for generating income, you can deduct travel expense based on Standard Mileage or based on actual expenditure. See 2018 Mileage rate.

Moving expense

In prior years, taxpayers could take a deduction for moving expenses incurred in connection with starting a new job or moving because of the job relocation if the new workplace was at least 50 miles away from the tax home and the taxpayer stayed put for the next 39 weeks-78 weeks. In the new tax bill, this deduction is repealed and any reimbursement for moving is taxable (except for members of the Armed Forces on active duty who move as a result of military order)

Not deductible in 2018: Moving expense for a new job - Car, transportation, meal, lodging, crating, and shipping .

Also: Nondeductible: refitting carpet, drapes, losses on sale of house, etc.

Tax Home and Work Location

A taxpayer's "tax home" is his principal place of work, *regardless of where he actually lives*. A taxpayer's tax home is used for tax purposes, including determining if travel expenses are deductible. Travel and meal expenses are considered deductible if the taxpayer is traveling away from her *tax home*. These rules are also used in determining if the taxpayer qualifies for the foreign earned income exclusion. Taxpayers with foreign accounts may need to complete various forms to show the taxability of the foreign income. For example, consider the following cases:

➤ Taxpayers with Foreign trust, IRS Form 3520.
➤ Foreign business, file IRS Form 5471.
➤ Holding a foreign bank account? They must file IRS Form 8938.

Multiple Work Locations (also see Tax Home)

If a taxpayer has *more than one* place of business or work, the tax home must be determined using several factors. The following facts should be used to determine which one is the main place of business or work:

- The total time ordinarily spent in each place
- The level of business activity in each place
- Whether income from each place is significant

In determining which is the "main place of business," the most important consideration is the length of time spent at each location.

 Example:

Ali is a marketing consultant who lives with his family in Chicago, but works regularly (full-time) in Milwaukee where he stays in a hotel and eats in restaurants. Ali returns to Chicago every weekend. Ali may not deduct any of his travel, meals, or lodging expenses in Milwaukee because that is his tax home. Ali's travel on weekends to his family home in Chicago is not for work, so these expenses are also not deductible.

If a taxpayer regularly works in more than one place, her tax home is the general area where the main place of business or work is located. If a taxpayer has *more than one* place of business, then her tax home is her *main* place of business. If a person does not have a regular place of business because of the nature of her work, then her tax home can be the place where she lives.

There are special rules for temporary work assignments. When a taxpayer is working away from his main place of business and the job assignment is temporary, his *tax home* does not change. The taxpayer can also deduct his travel expenses because the job assignment is of a temporary nature, and therefore, the travel is considered business-related.

***Special Note*: A temporary work assignment is any work assignment that is expected to last for *one year or less*. Travel expenses paid or incurred in connection with a temporary work assignment away from home are deductible. However, travel expenses paid in connection with an *indefinite* work assignment are *not deductible*. Any work assignment over one year in duration is considered *indefinite*. A taxpayer cannot deduct travel expenses at a work location if it is realistically expected that he will work there for more than one year.

There is an exception for federal crime investigations or prosecutions. If a taxpayer is a federal employee participating in a federal crime investigation or prosecution, he or she is not subject to the one year rule and may deduct travel expenses as long as the investigation takes place.

There is also a special rule for military personnel. Members of the armed forces on a permanent duty assignment overseas are not considered to be "traveling away from home." Therefore, members of the military cannot deduct their travel expenses for meals and lodging while on permanent duty assignment. However, military personnel that are permanently transferred from one duty station to another may be able to deduct their *moving expenses* as an adjustment to income (which will be explained in a later unit under Moving Expenses).

 Example:
Chico is a construction worker who lives and works primarily in Los Angeles. Chico is also a member of a trade union in Los Angeles that helps him get work in the Los Angeles area. Because of a shortage of work, Chico agrees to take a job on a construction site in Fresno. The Fresno job lasts ten months. Since the job lasts less than one year, the Fresno job is considered *temporary* and Chico's tax home is still in Los Angeles. Therefore, Chico's travel expenses are deductible since he was traveling away from his "tax home" for business or work. Chico can deduct travel expenses, *including* meals and lodging, while traveling between his temporary place of work and his tax home in Los Angeles (example in Publication 463).

Once a taxpayer has determined that she is traveling away from her *tax home*, she can deduct "ordinary and necessary" expenses incurred while traveling on business. Lodging, airline tickets, and meals are all examples of deductible travel expenses. If a taxpayer has an office in her home that qualifies as a principal place of business, she can deduct daily transportation costs between the home office and another work location in the same trade or business. Commuting expenses are never deductible. However, the travel between a home office to a business location would be considered deductible travel. The rules regarding home office expenses are covered more extensively in Part 2.

Example:

Theodore is a self-employed bookkeeper who works exclusively out of a home office. Theodore has many clients. Theodore travels from his home office directly to the client's business and performs his bookkeeping services on-site. Theodore does not have any other office. In this case, the travel from his home office to the client's location is deductible as business mileage.

Deductible Part of Self-Employment Tax

That part of SE tax you paid (If you filled Section A the amount will be on line 6 of Schedule SE. If you filed Section B, it is on line 13.)

Retirement Account

You may take a deduction for your contribution to self-Employed SEP, SIMPLE, and Qualified plans on Line 28, and any Health Insurance you paid for yourself, spouse and dependents (your child under the age of 27).or a partner (see pub 560 for detail). In 2017, payroll taxes are collected on income earned up to $127,200, but in 2018, they'll be collected on income up to $128,700 – (See more at ssa.gov),

Since Retirement Account consists of various scenarios, let's review them in more detail.

- IRA (Individual Retirement Arrangement)
- 401(k)
- 403(b) for schools, defense department, health
- 457, Government
- Deferral are 10% or under from your pay.
- SEP (Simplified Employee Pension Plan)
- SIMPLE 401 K

 IRA: Individual Retirement Arrangement: Traditional IRA is pre-tax. Roth IRA: Named after Senator Roth who proposed after tax contributions MAGI: Modified Adjusted Gross Income (see below)

How to calculate MAGI: Take AGI, and then add back:

- any deductions you took for IRA contributions
- any deductions you took for student loan interest or tuition
- half of your self-employment tax
- passive income or loss
- excluded foreign income
- rental losses
- interest from EE savings bonds used to pay higher education expenses, and
- employer-paid adoption expenses, and
- losses from a publicly-traded partnership

Retirement Plan Rules and their Limits

401(k), 403(b), 457, and Thrift Savings Plan contribution limits
For 2018, the contribution limit for employees into these types of accounts is rising from $18,000 to $18,500. For participants who will be age 50 and older by the end of 2018, the catch-up contribution amount of $6,000 (total of $24, 500) See www.fkianfa.com for updates every year.

In addition to the standard catch-up contribution limit, 403(b) plans can permit employees with at least 15 years of service to contribute as much as $3,000 more as part of their elective deferrals, even if they haven't reached age 50 yet. For employees over 50, **both** catch-up provisions can be used in many cases.

The IRA contribution limits. IRA owners can still contribute up to
$5,500 with an additional $1,000 catch-up contribution allowed for individuals age 50 or older. The contribution phase out for Single and HoH starts at $63,000 and the contribution is completely phased out at $73,000. For MFJ and QW the phase out is 101,000-$121,000 and for spouse$189,000-199,000. Contributions for the tax year is usually extended through the April of the following year (the Tax Day).

SEP-IRA limits

The SEP IRA is a retirement plan designed to benefit self employed individuals and small business owners. Sole proprietorships, S and C corporations, partnerships and LLCs qualify. Contributions to a SEP-IRA only come from the employer, and the maximum allowable contribution is 25% of each employee's salary up to the same

$55,000 maximum that applies to 401(k) and other workplace retirement plans as discussed in the first section.

For self-employed workers, who are also permitted to use a SEP-IRA to save for retirement, the effective contribution limit is reduced to 20% of adjusted profit after subtracting the self-employment tax, as the calculation is based on *net* self-employment income, which removes the SEP-IRA contribution itself.

SIMPLE IRA contribution limit

For 2018, the SIMPLE IRA employee contribution limit is unchanged at $12,500, with a $3,000 catch-up allowance for participants age 50 or older.

From the employer's side, there are two choices. The employer can choose to match their employees' contributions dollar-for-dollar up to 3% of their salaries with no limit, or can contribute 2% of every employee's salary regardless of whether the employees contribute or not, up to $5,500. The first option is potentially more lucrative for higher-earning employees, as it implies an overall maximum annual SIMPLE IRA contribution limit of $25,000 for employees under 50 or $31,000 for employees 50 or older.

Traditional IRA Deduction Income Limits

The IRS imposes income limits for those who are able to make a tax-deductible contribution to their Traditional IRA account. Those who earn less than a certain amount (detailed below) are able to deduct 100% of the contribution. There is a phase-out that allows participants to deduct a lesser amount than the full contribution level. The partial deduction can still be valuable, depending on your situation. Participants who have an Modified Adjusted Gross income greater than the highest level are not able to take a deduction on their contributions.

- **Single or Head of Household** can deduct the full amount of their contribution their MAGI is $63,000 or less. Deduction rates phase out beginning at a MAGI above $63,001, and end at $73,000 (up from $62,000, and $72,000, respectively in 2017). There is no tax deduction for those who have an income higher than $73,000.

- **Married Filing Jointly** can make maximum Traditional IRA contributions for an income of $101,000 or less. Traditional IRA eligibility ends at $121,000. (up from $99,000 and $119,000, respectively in 2017). There is no deduction for taxpayers who have an AGI of greater than $119,000.

- **Married Filing Separately** deductible contributions begin to phase-out with MAGI of $0, and are completely phased-out one MAGI exceeds $10,000.

Roth IRA Eligibility Income Limits

Like the Traditional IRA, the IRS has phase out rules for **Roth IRA** contributions. Tax filers will be able to contribute the maximum amount to their IRA if they don't exceed certain income limits.

- **Single or Head of Household** can contribute the maximum if their MAGI is $120,000 or less. Contribution rates phase out beginning at a MAGI above $120,001, and end at $135,000 (up from $118,000, and $133,000, respectively in 2017).

- **Married Filing Jointly** can make maximum Roth IRA contributions for an income of $189,000 or less. Roth IRA eligibility ends at $199,000. (up from $186,000 and $196,000, respectively in 2017).

- **Married Filing Separately** contributions begin to phase-out with MAGI of $0, and are completely phased-out one MAGI exceeds $10,000 just like the traditional IRA.

Direct Rollover by your Employer
- Rollover from other Retirement accounts to Roth IRA maybe taxable.
- If you directed the Employer to rollover of Partial and received a partial payment, that portion you received will be subject to 20% withholding
- Direct rollover is reported on 1099 R, box 1 but zero on Taxable amount on Box 2a. In box 7, G will be entered.

Personal Rollover
- If you receive distribution you will have 60 days to open a new Retirement account
- You will receive only 80% of the amount

- But the 100% will be entered in Box 1 of 1099
- Within 60 days you need to find another 20% from other sources to deposit 100% in your account.
- If you do not deposit the other 20%, that amount will be your taxable income.

Example:
1. John retires at age 52 with $100,000 which he instructs the employer to rollover. What is the tax withholdings?
2. He plans to receive the distribution. How much will he receive it?
3. He wants to deposit this to his IRA account. How long will he have time? How much does he need to deposit?
4. If he only deposited what he received, what is his additional taxable income?

Solution:
1. No tax impact
2. A 10% penalty for early withdrawal will apply (because he is under 59 ½ of age. He will receive $80,000 after that.
3. He has 60 days. Although he receives $80,000, he needs to deposit the whole $100,000
4. If he did deposit the $80,000, he needs to declare the other $20,000 as income

---

A 60 day deadline may be waived in extreme emergency cases --force majeure.

Surviving spouse (or divorced) may rollover to his or her retirement account to avoid early withdrawal penalty.

Retirement Accounts Summary

You can skip this part about IRA for a time being if you like, but retirement is one of the most important sections of IRS testing.

Traditional IRAs (Pretax Contribution)
In 2018, you can contribute up to $5,500 annually ($6,500 if you are 50 or older by the end of the year). However, if you or your spouse is covered by an employer retirement plan, this will affect how much, if any, of your contribution is tax-deductible. (See Publication 590, *Individual Retirement Arrangements)*. You can contribute to a traditional IRA even if you participate in an employer-sponsored retirement plan.

Roth IRAs (After Tax Contribution)

Here, you can contribute up to $5,500 ($6,500 if you are 50 or older by the end of the year). For 2014, you can make the maximum contribution to a Roth IRA if your filing status is married filing jointly and your MAGI is under $189,000.

You can also contribute to a Roth IRA even if you participate in an employer-sponsored retirement plan, but the amount you can contribute may be reduced or even eliminated depending on your modified adjusted gross income (MAGI) and your filing status. You cannot make a Roth IRA contribution for 2018 if your MAGI is $199,000 or more (See Pub. 590 for all the MAGI limits.)

The Florida Keys
KeyWest
Close To Perfect · Far From Normal

Contributing to both traditional and Roth IRAs

there is no limit on the number of Roth IRAs and traditional IRAs you can own; however, your combined annual contributions to all of them cannot exceed the maximum annual contribution limit ($5,000; $6,000 if 50 or older).

How can an individual convert a traditional IRA to a Roth IRA?

By this conversion you recharacterize the retirement account. A distribution from a traditional IRA can be contributed to a Roth IRA within 60 days after distribution. A conversion results in taxation of any untaxed amounts in the traditional IRA. Also, the conversion is reported on Form 8606, *Nondeductible IRAs*.

Taxpayers who convert a pre-tax traditional IRA into a post-tax Roth IRA lose their ability to later "re-characterize" (that is, reverse) the conversion. Those who wish to re-characterize a 2017 Roth conversion must do so by December 31, 2017.

Re-characterization is still an option for other contributions, though. For example, an individual can contribute to a Roth IRA and subsequently re-characterize it as a contribution to a traditional IRA (before the applicable deadline).

On January 18, 2018, IRS updated its FAQ pages to say that 2017 Roth IRA conversions could be recharacterized up to October 15, 2018. Following is the text from the IRS website.

How does the effective date apply to a Roth IRA conversion made in 2017?

A Roth IRA conversion made in 2017 may be recharacterized as a contribution to a traditional IRA if the recharacterization is made by October 15, 2018. A Roth IRA conversion made on or after January 1, 2018, cannot be recharacterized. For details, see "Recharacterization" in Publication 590-A, Contributions to Individual Retirement Arrangements (IRAs). Here is a link to the updated web page:

https://www.irs.gov/retirement-plans/ira-faqs-recharacterization-of-ira-contributions

The final bill generally retains the current rules for 401(k) and other retirement plans.

However, the bill repeals the rule allowing taxpayers to recharacterize Roth IRA contribution as Traditional IRA contributions to unwind a Roth conversion.

Plans report a direct rollover from a non-designated Roth account to a Roth IRA by stating:

a. the gross amount of the distribution in box 1;
b. the taxable amount of the rollover in box 2a;
c. any basis recovery amount in box 5; and
d. Code G in box 7.

Early distributions from the IRA

The IRA owner will need to file a Form 1040 and show the amount of withdrawal. If the withdrawal is taken before reaching age 59 1/2, (unless certain exceptions listed in Publication 590 *Individual Retirement Arrangements)*, the IRA owner will need to pay an additional 10% tax. (See Form 5329 *Additional Taxes on Qualified Plans).* This additional 10% tax on early distributions from qualified retirement plans does not qualify as a penalty for withdrawal of savings.

The Florida Keys
KeyWest
Close To Perfect · Far From Normal

Age 70 ½? Take Distribution!

If you were age 70½ or older at the end of the tax year, you cannot deduct any contributions made to your traditional IRA or treat them as nondeductible contributions.

Both the owner and any employees over age 70 1/2 must take required minimum distributions. Required minimum distributions apply each year beginning with the year the account owner turns age 70 1/2.

The required minimum distribution for each year is calculated by dividing the IRA account balance as of December 31 of the prior year by the applicable distribution period or life expectancy. An account owner can determine his or her applicable distribution period or life expectancy by using the Tables in Appendix C of Publication 590. Table I is used by beneficiaries. Table II is for use by owners who have spouses who are both the IRA's sole beneficiary and who are more than 10 years younger than the owner. Table III is for use by all other owners.

For example if you are 71, the life expectancy according to the publication 590 is 16.3, thus if the balance of IRA is $160,000, you must take approx. $10,000 for the year. If the taxpayer doesn't want to take the distribution, He/she can contribute to a qualified charitable distribution is a charitable gift:

- by an individual age 70½ or over
- paid directly from the individual's traditional or Roth IRA
- to a qualified charity

An individual does not include the amount of the qualified charitable distribution, up to $100,000, in gross income for the year for which it is made.

SIMPLE IRA Plan

A SIMPLE IRA plan (**S**avings **I**ncentive **M**atch **PL**an for **E**mployees) allows employees and employers to contribute to traditional IRAs set up for employees. It is ideally suited as a start-up retirement savings plan for small employers not currently sponsoring a retirement plan.

SIMPLE IRA plans can provide a significant source of income at retirement by allowing employers and employees to set aside money in retirement accounts. SIMPLE IRA plans do not have the start-up and operating costs of a conventional retirement plan.

- Available to any small business – generally with 100 or fewer employees
- Easily established by adopting Form 5304-SIMPLE, 5305-SIMPLE, a SIMPLE IRA prototype or an individually designed plan document
- Employer cannot have any other retirement plan
- No filing requirement for the employer
- Contributions:

- Employer is required to contribute each year either a:
  - Matching contribution up to 3% of compensation, or
  - 2% non-elective contribution for each eligible employee
- Employees may elect to contribute
- Employee is always 100% vested in (or, has ownership of) all SIMPLE IRA money

The following examples are right out of the IRS books:

 Example:
Elizabeth works for the Rockland Quarry Company, a small business with 50 employees. Rockland has decided to establish a SIMPLE IRA plan for its employees and will match its employees' contributions dollar-for-dollar up to 3% of each employee's compensation. Under this option, if a Rockland employee does not contribute to his or her SIMPLE IRA, then that employee does not receive any matching employer contribution.

Elizabeth has a yearly compensation of $50,000 and contributes 5% of her compensation ($2,500) to her SIMPLE IRA. The Rockland matching contribution is $1,500 (3% of $50,000). Therefore, the total contribution to Elizabeth's SIMPLE IRA that year is $4,000 (her $2,500 contribution plus Rockland's $1,500 contribution). The financial institution holding Elizabeth's SIMPLE IRA has several investment choices and she is free to choose which ones suit her best.

 Example:
Austin works for the Skidmore Tire Company, a small business with 75 employees. Skidmore has a SIMPLE IRA plan for its employees and will make a 2% non-elective contribution for each of them. Under this option, even if a Skidmore employee does not contribute to his or her SIMPLE IRA, that employee would still receive an employer contribution to his or her SIMPLE IRA equal to 2% of compensation.
Austin's annual compensation is $40,000. Even if Austin does not contribute this year, Skidmore must still make a contribution of $800 (2% of $40,000).

Contributions include:
1. salary reduction contributions and
2. employer contributions: a. matching contributions or b. nonelective contributions.

No other contributions can be made to a SIMPLE IRA plan.

 Salary reduction contributions

The amount the employee contributes to a SIMPLE IRA cannot exceed $12,500 for 2018 **Catch-up contributions**. If permitted by the SIMPLE IRA plan, participants who are age 50 or over at the end of the calendar year can also make catch-up contributions. The catch-up contribution limit for SIMPLE IRA plans is $3,000.

The maximum annual SIMPLE IRA contribution limit of $25,000 for employees under 50 or $31,000 for employees 50 or older.

Generally, all elective deferrals that you make to all plans in which you participate **must be considered to determine if the dollar limits are exceeded**. Limits on the amount of elective deferrals that you can contribute to a SIMPLE 401(k) plan are different from those in a traditional or safe harbor 401(k).

Although, general rules for 401(k) plans provide for the dollar limit described above, that does not mean that you are entitled to defer that amount. Other limitations may come into play that would limit your elective deferrals to a lesser amount. For example, your plan document may provide a lower limit or the plan may need to further limit your elective deferrals in order to meet nondiscrimination requirements.

Participation in plans of unrelated employers

If you participate in plans of different employers, you can treat amounts as catch-up contributions regardless of whether the individual plans permit those contributions. In this case, it is up to you to monitor your deferrals to make sure that they do not exceed the applicable limits.

Example:
If Chico Saver, who's over 50, has only one employer and participates in that employer's 401(k) plan, the plan would have to permit catch-up contributions before he could defer the maximum of $24,500 for 2018 (the $18,500 regular limit for 2018 plus the $6,000 catch-up limit for 2018). If the plan didn't permit catch-up contributions, the most Chico could defer would be $24,500.

The rules relating to catch-up contributions are complex and your limits may differ according to provisions in your specific plan. You should contact your plan administrator to find out whether your plan allows catch-up contributions and how the catch-up rules apply to you.

Treatment of excess deferrals

If the total of your elective deferrals is more than the limit, you can have the difference (called an excess deferral) returned to you from any of the plans that permit these distributions. You must notify the plan by April 15 of the following year of the amount to be paid from the plan. The plan must then pay you that amount plus allocable earnings by April 15 of the year following the year in which the excess occurred.

Excess withdrawn by April 15

If you withdraw the excess deferral, it is includable in your gross income. The April 15 date is not tied to the due date for your return and is not extended until April15, 2015. However, any income earned on the excess deferral taken out is taxable in the tax year in which it is taken out. The distribution is not subject to the additional 10% tax on early distributions.

Excess not withdrawn by April 15

If you do not take out the excess deferral by April 15, the excess, though taxable prior year, is not included in your cost basis in figuring the taxable amount of any eventual distributions from the plan. In effect, **an excess deferral left in the plan is taxed twice**, once when contributed and again when distributed. Also, if the entire deferral is allowed to stay in the plan, the plan may not be a qualified plan.

 **Simplified Employee Pension Plan (SEP)**

A SEP plan allows employers to contribute to traditional IRAs (SEP-IRAs) set up for employees. A business of any size, even self-employed, can establish a SEP.

A SEP does not have the start-up and operating costs of a conventional retirement plan and allows **for a contribution of up to 25 percent of each employee's pay.**
- Available to any size business
- Easily established by adopting Form 5305-SEP, a SEP prototype or an individually designed plan document

- If Form 5305-SEP is used, cannot have any other retirement plan (except another SEP)
- No filing requirement for the employer
- Only the employer contributes
    - To traditional IRAs (SEP-IRAs) set up for each eligible employee
    - Employee is always 100% vested in (or, has ownership of) all SEP-IRA money

 Example:
Jed works for the Rambling RV Company. Rambling RV decides to establish a SEP for its employees. Rambling RV has chosen a SEP because the RV industry is cyclical in nature, with good times and down times. In good years, Rambling RV can make larger contributions for its employees and in down times it can reduce the amount. Rambling RV's contribution rate (whether large or small) must be uniform for all employees. The financial institution that Rambling RV has chosen for its SEP has several investment funds from which to choose. Jed decides to divide the contribution to his SEP-IRA among three of the available funds. Jed, an employee, cannot contribute because SEPs only permit employer contributions.

Pros and Cons for SEP Plan:
- Easy to set up and operate
- Low administrative costs
- Flexible annual contributions – good plan if cash flow is an issue
- Employer must contribute equally for all eligible employees

You may want to make a suggestion to your taxpayer who wants to withdraw… Instead of withdrawal, take a loan out of your own retirement account. You have to pay it back in years and the interest is what you give to yourself.

Maximum Loan Amount

The maximum amount a participant may borrow from his or her plan is 50% of his or her vested account balance or $50,000, whichever is less. An exception to this limit is if 50% of the vested account balance is less than $10,000: in such case, the participant may borrow up to $10,000. Plans are not required to include this exception.

Example:
Bill's vested account balance is $80,000. Bill may take a loan up to $40,000, which is the lesser of 50% of his vested account balance and $50,000.
Sue has a vested account balance of $120,000. Sue may take a loan up to $50,000, which is the lesser of 50% of her vested account balance of $120,000 ($60,000) or $50,000.

Repayment Periods

Generally, the employee must repay a plan loan within five years and must make payments at least quarterly. The law provides an exception to the 5-year requirement if the employee uses the loan to purchase a primary residence.

Loans to an employee that leaves the company

Plan sponsors may require an employee to repay completely a loan if he or she terminates employment. If the employee is unable to repay the loan, then the employer will treat it as a distribution and will report it to the IRS on Form 1099-R. The employee can avoid the immediate income tax consequences if he or she is able to come up with the loan's outstanding balance, within 60 days and rolls over this amount to an IRA or eligible retirement plan.

Alimony

If you are deducting Alimony to get to your AGI, enjoy it while it lasts because coming January 2019, ***Alimony is no longer deductible for the payer spouse or taxable for the recipient spouse.*** This could have a significant effect on negotiations in equitable distribution agreements. Understanding the effect of this dramatic change in the tax implications of alimony is important. If you currently are receiving or paying alimony, your current agreement may be modified with certain specific language to comply with the new tax rule.

The bill repeals the deduction for alimony payments and their inclusion in the income of the recipient. To give taxpayers time to adjust to this new balance in assessing benefits and burdens, the TCJA will apply only to divorce or separation instruments executed after December 31, 2018.

Payments are Alimony if all of the Following are True

1. Payments are required by a divorce or separation instrument
2. Payer and recipient spouse do not file a joint return with each other
3. Payment is in cash (including checks) or payment is made using money orders
4. Payment is **not** designated in the instrument as **not alimony**
5. Spouses legally separated under a decree of divorce or separate maintenance are not members of the same household
6. Payments are not required after death of the recipient spouse
7. Payment is not treated as child support

These payments are deductible by the payer and includible in income by the recipient.

 ## Payments are NOT alimony if any of the following are true:

1. Payments are not required by a divorce or separation instrument
2. Payer and recipient spouse file a joint return with each other
3. Payment is:
   - Not in cash
   - A noncash property settlement
   - Spouse's part of community income
   - To keep up the payer's property
4. Payment **is** designated in the instrument as not alimony
5. Spouses legally separated under a decree of divorce or separate maintenance are members of the same household
6. Payments are required after death of the recipient spouse
7. Payment is treated as child support

Student Loan Interest Deduction at a Glance

Loan qualifications for your student loan:
- Must have been taken out solely to pay qualified education expenses
- Cannot be from a related person or made under a qualified employer plan.

Student Qualifications - The student must be:
- You, your spouse, or your independent

- Enrolled at least half-time in a degree program
- A dependent when the loan was made

Time limit on deduction - You can deduct interest paid during the remaining period of your student loan

Phase-out - The amount of your deduction depends on your income level

- **Credit Amount:** up to $2,500 of the cost of tuition, fees and course materials paid during the taxable year **per eligible student**.

- **How to Claim:** Determine your eligibility, credit amount, and claim the credit by filling out **IRS Form 8863**. New this year: To claim the American opportunity credit, you must provide the educational institution's employer identification number (EIN) on your Form 8863. You should also file form **1098-T**, which you should receive early in the year from your educational institution.

- **Refundability:** 40% of the credit (up to $1,000) is refundable. This means you can get a refund even if you owe no tax.

Income Limits: a taxpayer whose **modified adjusted gross income**:

- $80,000 or less ($160,000 or less for joint filers) can claim the credit for the qualified expenses of an eligible student. The credit is reduced if a taxpayer's modified adjusted gross income exceeds those amounts.

- A taxpayer whose modified adjusted gross income is greater than $90,000 ($180,000 for joint filers) cannot claim any of the credit.

- **School Eligibility:** You can only claim the credit if you're attending an accredited institutions. You can search the U.S. Department of Education's database of **accredited institutions** to confirm eligibility.

- **Credit can be received for:** Tax credit can be received for 100% of the first $2,000, plus 25% of the next $2,000 that has been paid during the taxable year for tuition, and required fees and course materials.

- **Ineligible Expenses:** You cannot receive a credit for: room and board, insurance, transportation, expenses paid with tax-free assistance, medical expenses, expenses used for another deduction or credit, and student fees that are not required as condition of enrollment or attendance.

Student Loan Interest Deduction Worksheets

Generally, you figure the deduction using the *Student Loan Interest Deduction Worksheet* in Form 1040 or Form1040A instructions. However, if you are filing Form 2555, 2555-EZ, or 4563, or you are excluding income from Puerto Rico, you must complete *Worksheet 4-1* in Publication 970. Most software will calculate the deduction based on the filing status and income limits.

Tuition and Fees

If you paid qualified tuition and fees for yourself, your spouse, or your dependent(s), see form 8917. If it's not possible for you to take this credit, then you may be able to take advantage of Education Credit (on Line 49 of 1040) and use Form is 8863.

Domestic Production Activities Deduction

Up to 9% credit if qualified for:

1- Construction of real property performed in the United States
2- Engineering or architectural services performed in the United States for construction of real property.
3- Any lease, rental, license, sale, exchange, or other disposition of:
   a. Tangible personal property, computer software, and sound recording that you manufactured, produced, grew or extracted in the United States.
   b. Any qualified film you produced, or
   c. Electricity, natural gas, or potable water you produced

The deduction does not apply to income derived from:
   a. The sale of food and beverages you prepared at a retail establishment
   b. Property you leased, licensed or rented for use by any related person;

LET'S DO A LITTLE QUIZ TO INCLUDE GROSS INCOME AND
REDUCTIONS:

Example: Calculate the AGI

1-	W2 Income	$10,000
2-	Federal taxes paid	$4,500
3-	Interest income	$1,200
4-	1099 received from contracts	$22,000
5-	Taxable fringe benefits received	$1,500
6-	IRA Contribution	$4,500
7-	Self-employed insurance paid	$12,000
8-	HSA contribution	$4,000
9-	Moving expense to another city*	$1,800
10-	Transfer of property from spouse	$45,000
11-	Sold this property at	$55,000
12-	Purchased another property for	$50,000

13- Purchased 1,000 stocks from your company (worth $25) that cost you $22 each

14- Paid 2,600 for gas travelling from home to work for the year

- **Moving expense is eliminated in 2018, and here it shows just in case you had a 2017 tax client.**
- **Remember about the Self Employment tax for the 1099.**

Solutions:

W2				
	Income	10,000		
	Tax paid	0		
	Int. Income	1,200		
	Contract-1099	22,000		
	Fringe benefits	1,500		
	Capital Gain	10,000		
	Other income	3,000		
Total Income		47,700		
Deductions	IRA contribution			4,500
	Self Employed ins			12,000
	HSA			4,000
	Moving Expense			1,800
	½ SE tax*			1,683
Total Adjustment				23,983
AGI				$23,817

- **Remember to include ½ of the self- employment tax in adjustments.**

Reference material:

Unit 1.1: Preliminary Work and Individual Taxpayer Data
IRS publication 1040, Publication 17, *Your Federal Income Tax*
More Reading:
Publication 519, *U.S. Tax Guide for Aliens*

Section IV: BELOW THE LINE DEDUCTIONS

Chapter VII: Exemptions and Deductions

The deduction for personal exemptions is eliminated in 2018 as well as the personal exemption phase-out (through 2025). If you had to remember two types of below the line deductions such as "standard or itemized deductions" as well as "exemptions" to reduce the AGI and to get to the taxable amount, remember, there's no more personal exemptions in 2018. Perhaps the main reason that the standard deduction is increased is to get rid of Exemption.

Personal exemptions was scheduled to be $4,100 in 2018* (See yearly updates at fkianfa.com/updates.)

Generally there are many forms of exemptions:

1. Personal exemptions - one exemption for the taxpayer and, if married, one for his or her spouse unless they can be claimed as a dependent by another person.

2. Exemption for dependents - one exemption for each qualifying child or qualifying relative.
3. Exemptions for AMT
4. Exemption for Gift and Estate Taxes

Form 1040

Tax and Credits	38	Amount from line 37 (adjusted gross income) . . .				38	
	39a	Check if: ☐ You were born before January 2, 1947, ☐ Blind. Total boxes					
		☐ Spouse was born before January 2, 1947, ☐ Blind. checked ▶ 39a					
Standard Deduction for—	b	If your spouse itemizes on a separate return, check here ▶ 39b☐					
	40	Itemized deductions (from Schedule A) or your standard deduction (see left margin) . .				40	
• People who check any box on line 39a or 39b or who can be claimed as a dependent, see instructions.	41	Subtract line 40 from line 38				41	
	42	Exemptions.				42	
	43	Taxable income. Subtract line 42 from line 41. If line 42 is more than line 41, enter -0- . . .				43	
	44	Tax (see instructions). Check if any from: a ☐ Form(s) 8814 b ☐ Form 4972 c ☐ 962 election				44	
	45	Alternative minimum tax (see instructions). Attach Form 6251 . . .				45	
• All others:	46	Add lines 44 and 45 . . . . ▶				46	
Single or Married filing separately, $5,800	47	Foreign tax credit. Attach Form 1116 if required	47				
	48	Credit for child and dependent care expenses. Attach Form 2441	48				
	49	Education credits from Form 8863, line 23	49				
Married filing jointly or Qualifying widow(er), $11,600	50	Retirement savings contributions credit. Attach Form 8880	50				
	51	Child tax credit (see instructions)	51				
	52	Residential energy credits. Attach Form 5695	52				
Head of household, $8,500	53	Other credits from Form: a ☐ 3800 b ☐ 8801 c ☐	53				
	54	Add lines 47 through 53. These are your **total credits**				54	
	55	Subtract line 54 from line 46. If line 54 is more than line 46, enter -0- . . . . . ▶				55	

Copy to Use for Example
Kianfa study guide

Exemptions used to live here! Line 42.
Also see the side bar for the amounts of
standard deductions in line 40

Deductions

The standard deduction is almost doubled: The standard deduction is

$24,000 for married individuals filing a joint return,

$18,000 for head-of-household filers, and

$12,000 for all other individuals,

Indexed for inflation (using chained CPI) for tax years beginning after 2018.

All increases are temporary and would end after December 31, 2025.

Before the tax reform, the standard deductions for 2018 had been set at $13,000 for joint filers, $9,550 for head of household and $6,500 for all other filers.

Then additional standard deduction for the elderly and the blind

$1,300 for married taxpayers,

$1,600 for single taxpayers) is retained in the new tax law.

One major goal of a higher standard deduction is to simplify tax through cutting the number of those taxpayers who would otherwise do better by itemizing their deductions to half. Of course, that group would realize less of a tax benefit than those taxpayers who do not now itemize. Supporters argue that, in addition to the simplification, it effectively creates a more broadly applicable "zero tax bracket" for the tax payer. The doubling of the standard deduction would effectively illuminate most individuals from claiming itemize deductions other than higher-income tax payers. Maybe less focus on the audit of Schedule A, can help IRS to audit other schedules.

For example,

For the vast majority of MFJ, Only those with allowable mortgage interest, state income, and local income/property taxes (up to $10,000), and charitable deductions that exceed $24,000 would claim them
as itemized deductions (absent extraordinary medical expenses). With fewer individuals claiming those deductions, this could have a great impact on both the real estate prices and charitable organizations-despite retaining those two deductions, and modified formers earning less than the standard deduction amount.

The followings summarizes the expenses, but, again, before you go through itemizing ever item, see if they are higher than the percentages of AGI as you can see in the parenthesis below:

 **Itemized Deductions**

1. **Medical and dental expenses:** is it more than 7.5% in 2018 and 10% of your AGI (if less, don't itemize) starting in 2019 going forward.
2. **Real estate taxes, and city and state taxes**
3. **Mortgage interest expense** (e.g., Form 1098 Mortgage Interest Statement)
4. **Charitable contributions** (e.g., cash, non-cash, Form 8283 Non-Cash Charitable Contributions)
5. **Casualty and theft:** add up all sudden losses due to theft or casualties minus $100; is the total more than 10% of your AGI? (if not, you may not benefit from itemizing - see more detail on casualty computation)
6. **Miscellaneous itemized deductions:** such as unreimbursed travel, transportation, education, and entertainment expenses. Most of these items are not accepted in 2018 due to the new tax reform and most others will be heavily audited (e.g., Form 2106-EZ and Form 2106 Unreimbursed Employee Business Expenses if more than 2% AGI)

Medical and Dental Expenses

Medical out of pocket exceeding 7.5% in 2018 and 10% of your AGI in 2019 are deductible.

- Premium, doctor fees, prescription medicine, related travel cost, and even home improvement for health.
- If married and both of you work, and one has substantial medical expense, file separately

Monthly service fees paid to retirement community for lifetime care is deductible. So are the followings:

- Contact lenses and solutions
- Teaching or learning of Braille and lip reading
- Educational courses to overcome disability
- 100% of premium paid by self-employed are deductible (from gross income)

> **Example:**
> We are looking only at the Medical portion of Itemized Deductions: You are single and your AGI is $60,000. You have collected all your medical bills and it adds up to $8,000 in eligible medical expensed that your insurance hasn't paid for. Would you itemize your medical?
> How about total of all your receipt for taxes, interest, and charitable contribution added up to $15,200 and you are filing as Head of a Household with an AGI of $60,000?

Residential Taxes

You can itemize personal taxes and real estate taxes you have paid. You also can deduct these taxes on Schedule A.

- Real estate taxes
- Assessments
- Automobile license fees
- Excise taxes aside from these: Alcohol, cigarette, gas, gift taxes, inheritance, social security, tolls, transfer securities are deductible.
- Itemize deductible state and local taxes (income and property)

Special Note: Deduct EITHER state and local taxes *OR* state and local general tax, not both (Line 5 schedule A box a OR b)

Cutting down on SALT (State and local tax deduction)

Maybe it's the red-meat-thing but the bill limits the local taxes which includes state and local income, sales, real estate, or property taxes combined to $10,000. This is one act that may impact those taxpayers in high taxed states.

Mortgage Interest Deduction

Interest on purchases and refinance are deductible:

- Must be secured by residence
- Up to two residences qualify - if you have more, you need to decide which will be your second residence
- Home acquisition loan is about $500,000 for single filer
- Home equity loans can be used for other purposes but up to $100,000 of it can be used for interest deduction.
- Points (generally prepaid interest) are ratable in accordance to the life of the loan

If these tests are met, points are paid on the year paid:

- Loan is secured by principal residence
- Charging points is an established business practice in your area.
- Points charges does not exceed the generally charged points in the area
- Marked in closing document as points
- Points are paid directly to the lender.

Special Note: Generally a $1,200 point for a 10 year loan: 1200/120=10 a month
- Investment interest is accrued on debts incurred to buy properties (except tax exempt securities)
- Deduct interests paid for investment up to the interest income and no more. No investment income = no interest deducted.

To compute: add investment income (dividends, annuities, royalties, etc.) and subtract expenses taken into account, 2% floor (see further down, miscellaneous deductions).

In the new tax law (TCJA) Mortgage interest is deductible to buy, build or improve the taxpayer's home. When you own a home (or vice versa), you are more anchored, and would stay at your job, which is very good for the economy. TCJA repeals the deduction for home equity indebtedness (currently up to $100,000) but will keep the deduction for acquisition indebtedness at the current level of up to $1 million for mortgages taken out before December 15, 2017. After this date, the mortgage interest deduction will be capped at $750,000. On the other hand, one of the most important considerations in buying a home for many taxpayers is the deductibility of mortgage interest and taxes. The TCJA didn't change much for mortgages you may have if it's under $750,000. The interest on your mortgage is tax deductible. Of course, if you want to be more stable and purchase a house over this amount, you can only deduct up to the interest of $750,000 mortgage.

Meanwhile... interest on home equity loans used for purposes other than to improve the current home, will not be deductible after 2017. For those taxpayers, whose home mortgage is above $750,000, that they'd just like to itemize as an unwritten principle, they may still do so by itemization if they donate handsomely to charitable organizations. Please see https://www.irs.gov/newsroom/interest-on-home-equity-loans-often-still-deductible-under-new-law

Example: In August 2018, a taxpayer takes out a $400,000 mortgage to purchase the main home. The loan is secured by the main home. In October 2018, the taxpayer takes out a $250,000 loan to purchase a vacation home. The loan is secured by the main home. What part of the Mortgage interest is deductible?

> **Answer:** Since the taxpayer took out a $250,000 home equity loan on the main home to purchase another home, (the vacation home), then the interest on the home equity loan would not be deductible.

Example: A TP purchased home for $300,000 (acquisition indebtedness). After 3 years, the balance on the loan is $290,000 and TP decides to refinance it for $350,000, but the deductible portion of the debt new loan is that same, $290,000. The other $60,000 is not deductible.

Charitable Contributions

In a nutshell, chances are most small donors will not benefit from itemizing their deductions because the standard deduction is raised from $6,400 to $12,000 for a single taxpayer, so if they don't have major donations, there's little reason to itemize.

60% AGI limit for cash contributions

If one is giving out of the goodness in his (her) heart and helping people in need, it is one thing, but I understand many people think of giving to charities in order to reduce their taxes. Well, that's also a school of thought (which may or may not offer a degree). In prior years, the taxpayers can give up to 50% of their AGI to the 50% organizations (churches, schools, and all those Exempt organizations that get 1/3 of their funding from public support) but let's be clear, in the often seen emotionally charged advertising where they claim that your donation is a 100% deductible. It's not. Your donation depends on your tax rate. For instance, the higher your tax bracket, the greater is your tax savings as a result of making charitable contributions. For example, if a donor in the 37% tax bracket makes a donation of $10,000, this person may reduce their taxable income by $3,700 in savings. However, if he were in the 12% tax bracket, his $10,000 would drain only $1,200 of his tax liabilities. Frankly, if that person who is actually making under $20,000, gives $10,000 to charities just to reduce their tax liabilities, I would suggest they look into their medical deductions first as the mean for higher deductions and instead of charities, get their head examined first. Although it's not stressed what type of organization can receive the 60% this still falls on the same path as the 50% organizations (like religious and educational organizations).

Yet, taxpayers may have better charitable deductions with the TCJA that has enhanced the charitable contributions by raising the limit that can be contributed in any one year. The limit is now 60% of adjusted gross income, up from 50%. So if MFJ and in 10% bracket and make about $20,000 in AGI, you can still donate $12,000 in charities and may still manage to stay married. With the same token, A credit, such as Education credit can reduce tax liability and generate refund much better than charitable contribution because as we saw Charitable contribution is a Deduction that saves you based on your tax bracket, but Education Credit reduces your tax liability dollar for dollar.

The charitable giving deduction remains for taxpayers who itemize. Under the new law, this break is limited to 60 percent of adjusted gross income for cash gifts, but you can carry forward by up to five years any amount that exceeds that.

For example, suppose in 2017 a taxpayer who files as Single, has itemized deductions of $10,350, or $4,000 more than the standard deduction of $6,350. Suppose, in 2018 this taxpayer, again has $10, 400 in expenses that would have been deductible in 2017. With a new, higher standard deduction of $12,000, the taxpayer will not benefit from itemizing, although people have by now gotten used to keeping receipts for tax time. If they are in lower income bracket, 'Tis the season to help them forget minor deductions.

Nondeductible contributions:

- Donations or scholarship for a specific student
- Payment to PACMEN (Political Action Committee)
- Gift to fraternity or sorority group unless aimed for charitable and educational (20-30%)
- Civic leagues, communist organizations, chambers of commerce, business leagues
- Contribution to charitable organization in foreign countries
- Volunteer work

30% or 60% to Charitable Organizations:
Donation of your AGI to these organizations is 60%
- Churches
- Colleges
- Hospitals
- Private foundations
- Organizations that receive 1/3 of their funding from government or public supported organization (receiving 1/3 of their income from public contribution)

30% ceiling for donation of property with long term capital gain to the 60% organizations

20% - 30% Organizations:
- Veterans' organizations
- Fraternal societies
- Nonprofit cemeteries
- 20% of AGI for property with long term gain to non 60% org.

Contributions that Provide Benefits to You:
- Benefit tickets
- Donations for the right to buy athletic stadium tickets (80% deductible), but if you exercised your rights and bought tickets, subtract the value of tickets
- All contributions to charitable organizations that may offer Low-Cost-Articles (mugs, bags, and anything under $9.50)

Quick Notes
- ✓ If you are in a 12% bracket, your $1,000 giving reduces your taxes by $120
- ✓ For donation of $250 or more you need proof cancelled check is not a proof)
- ✓ If you gave over $500, you must attach cop B of 1098-C and complete 8283
- ✓ If they sold it for less, you need to recapture your deduction

TCJA 2017 Repeal to contemporaneous written acknowledgment

In previous years, a written acknowledgment as shown in publication 526 was required to substantiate a charitable contribution of $250 or more and the acknowledgment had to show the information below:

- Name of the organization;

- Amount of cash contribution;

- Description (but not value) of non-cash contribution;

- Statement that no goods or services were provided by the organization, if that is the case;

- Description and good faith estimate of the value of goods or services, if any, that organization provided in return for the contribution; and

- Statement that goods or services, if any, that the organization provided in return for the contribution consisted entirely of intangible religious benefits if that was the case.

Accordingly, a donor could claim a deduction for contributions of cash, check, or other monetary gifts only if the donor maintains certain written records. The new law eliminates the alternative gift substantiation, which—in certain cases allows—the receiving organization to file a separate document with its annual IRS return rather than provide a contemporaneous gift receipt to donors for contributions exceeding $250 (effective for taxable years beginning after December 31, 2016).

 Problem:

You have heard the tax advantage of charitable contributions, so let's figure how much we will save if....

1. You are in a 22% tax bracket. How much is your tax reduced if you pay $10,000 to a charitable organization?
2. You are in a 12% tax bracket and you donate $1,000.

Solution:
Multiply the percentage of the tax bracket by the donation amount.
1. 22% x $10,000 = $2,200
2. 12% x $1,000 = $120

Volunteer Work

These are the deductibles:

- Car expense, gas, and transportation ($0.14 per mile)
- Up to $250 donation is deductible; receipt for extra amount

Expenses for "recreational travels" (although for charitable volunteering) is not deductible; e.g. if you are in a meeting or seminar in a room for 10 hours you can deduct, but if you are counting whales or dolphins for an environmental agency you cannot. Please see updated number for each year at the beginning of this Study Guide.

Think about these examples:

Example:

Betty owns securities that cost her $20,000 when she bought it several years ago but now it is worth $5,000. Should she sell it and donate $5,000 in cash or should she donate it as it is?

If you give away your car and deduct $500 and the charitable organization sold it for $700, what is the value of your charitable contribution?
How if they sold it for $300? How would it impact you?

Problem:

You are married with two children, filing jointly. You have qualified medical deductions of $4,400 and your AGI is $53,000. Is it beneficial for taxpayer to use standard deduction?

Problem:

Same as above and taxpayer is head of a household.

Problem:

Insurance payment next year:

Your AGI is $32,000 and medical expenses incurred are $3,800.
1.   How much are you assumed to have as standard for medical return?
In 2019, you received $500 from 2018 insurance expenses.
2.   How do you account for this?

Casualty and Theft Losses

Taxpayers will only be able to deduct a casualty loss if it occurs in a disaster that is declared by the president because he alone can know a disaster.

A disaster loss is actually a casualty loss that occurs in a geographic area that the President of the United States declares eligible for deduction. Needless to say, a casualty loss occurs when there is property damage from a sudden, unanticipated event. Some examples of qualifying events are hurricanes, earthquakes, tornadoes, floods, storms, fire and volcanic eruptions. You may deduct the damages over 10% of your AGI with a floor of $100 deductible per event.

The TCJA outlines when a casualty is deductible: A taxpayer in a federally declared disaster area can claim a casualty loss either on their return for the year of the loss or on their return for the previous year. If the previous year's return has already been filed, as is generally the case, it can be amended by filing a Form 1040X.

You can get a little panicked if Big Brother is not watching you when you went to the kitchen to scramble an egg and set the place on fire, and it's advisable to avoid the kitchen for the year after you filed the loss, because you may not be able to deduct this loss once the bill is fine-tuned. Although the title of this deduction is casualty and theft, I suppose it's only the IRS trying to maintain certain consistency with the old traditions because I didn't see any clear idea on how theft is covered in the TCJA. So, it's best to calmly check some of the anti-theft devices online because this may not be a qualified deduction once they got this Act together.

Summary for Casualty and Theft Losses:

- Use form 4684
- Sudden event: natural disaster, vandalism, accident, and even damage to trees
- This year it must be substantial due to reduction of $100 and 10% reduction in disaster areas.
- Income-producing purposes (goes to line 28 of schedule A)

- Kidnapping ransom is deductible
- Business theft (although on 4684, also need Form 4797)

Non-Deductible Losses:
- Termite,
- Loss of property in storage
- Loss of dog who strayed away
- Damage to crop caused by diseases
- Moth damage,
- Damage from rust

 Computing Casualty

1) Find the loss in <u>fair market value</u> appraised professionally or use <u>basis</u> for property valuation
2) Pick the lower one of the two from above.
3) Reduce the result with insurance payment
4) Subtract $100 from losses. This is called Floor Amount from here forth.
5) 10% of your AGI

<u>Think about this:</u>
If you have 5 events of casualties in a year ($1,000, $2,000, $3,000, $1,000, and $2,000, how much can you claim? Contrast this with one event at $9,000 damage.

If you had one event of $3,000 casualty how much can you claim?

Problem:
In January you had an uninsured jewelry loss of $1,400 and in July a damage of $5,400 on your car. Your AGI is $45,000. How much can you claim?

Solution:

Theft loss:	$1,400	
Less: floor $	100	
First event	1300	
Car damage		5,400
Less: floor amount		100

This event:	5,300	
Total loss		6600
Minus: 10% AGI		4,500
Deductible:		$2100

Job Expenses

Up to 2017 Schedule A accepted the unreimbursed travels, union fees, uniform costs, job education, food and entertainment, cost of looking for a job, PC, cell phone bought for work, and any meal and entertainment after 50% reduction. Some of the job expenses included:

- Use computer for one's job duties.
- All payments you made to attend seminars, conferences fees as well as education enrollment for which the business did not reimburse employee.
- Tax preparation fee
- Investment expenses, safe deposit box
- Subscriptions to upkeep your proficiencies at the job
- Use this if the miscellaneous expenses were deductible if they exceeded 2% of one's AGI
- Other unreimbursed employee expenses such as plane, train, taxi, hotel, meal, tips, phone, laundry, etc.

Not Deductible: Commuting to work daily

Deductible: Temporary work travel (to employer for 2-3 weeks)
Meal and lodging (50%) if over 8 hours away from your work and away from home
Travel expense if you are going straight form one job to the next.

 Problem:
Your AGI is $50,000. You paid:
   Investment management fees = $1,500
   Tax preparation fee = $500
   Safe deposit box = $50
   Other misc. = $300
What is your deduction and where does it go?

Chapter VIII: Alternative Minimum Tax (AMT)

Form 1040 — Page 2 — Tax and Credits (lines 38–55). Circled annotation: "Copy to Use for Example Kianfa study guide"

The alternative minimum tax (AMT)- (which is only a parallel tax system) was designed to prevent high-income taxpayers from avoiding tax liability by using various exclusions, deductions, and credits. Therefore AMT is not an additional tax and it's often called a Parallel Tax.

A taxpayer pays either the AMT tax or the traditional tax based on tax bracket—whichever is higher. Although individual exemptions are gone away on the regular taxes, the AMT still is subject to the exemptions. Once the taxpayer's AMTI is calculated, we deduct the exemption and the result is multiplied by 26% or 28% depending on the threshold—described below.

For 2018, the AMT exemption amounts <u>WERE scheduled</u> to be:

- $86,200 for marrieds filing jointly/surviving spouses (FMS will take half of this exemption)
- $55,400 for other unmarried individuals;

For income higher than the Phaseout amount, those exemption amounts were reduced by an amount equal to 25% of the amount by which the individual's AMTI exceeded the threshold amounts shown below:

- $164,100 for marrieds filing jointly and surviving spouses (phase-out complete at $508,900); MFS will be $82,050 (phase-out complete at $180,450).
- $123,100 for unmarried individuals (phase-out complete at $344,700);

Additionally, the married person filing must add the lesser of the following to AMTI: (1) 25% of the excess of AMTI (determined without regard to this adjustment) over the minimum amount of income at which the exemption will be completely phased out, or (2) the exemption amount. So, for 2018, married people filing separately must add the lesser of the following to AMTI: (1) 25% of the excess of AMTI over $254,450, or $43,100.

For trusts and estates, for 2018, the exempt amount was scheduled to be $24,600, and the exemption was to be reduced by 25% of the amount by which its AMTI exceeded $82,050 (phase-out complete at $254,450).

MEANWHILE...

Under TCJA, the AMT exemption amount is increased significantly, as well as the threshold for the phase-out of the AMT exemption. In effect, this means that vastly fewer households will be subject to the AMT over the coming years. However, this change is set to expire after December 31, 2025, meaning that far more households would be subject to the AMT after 2025.

For tax years from 2018 through 2025, the Act increases the AMT exemption amounts for individuals as follows:

Under the Act, the above exemption amounts are reduced (not below zero) to an amount equal to 25% of the amount by which the AMTI of the taxpayer exceeds the phase-out amounts, increased as follows:

To summarize:

Filing Status	AMT Exemption Amount	AMT Phase-out Income Level
2018 AMT Thresholds and Exemptions in TCJA		
Single	$70,300	$500,000
Joint Returns or Widow (er)	$109,400	$1,000,000

2017 AMT Thresholds and Exemptions by Filing Status

Single	$54,300	$120,700
Joint Returns or Surviving Spouses	$84,500	$160,900

In 2018, the 28 percent AMT rate applies to excess AMTI of $191,500 for all married taxpayers $95,750 for unmarried individuals.

Under the TCJA, AMT exemptions phase out at 25 cents per dollar earned once taxpayer AMTI hits a certain threshold. In 2018, the exemption will start phasing out at $500,000 in AMTI for single filers and $1 million for married taxpayers filing jointly

Filing Status	Threshold
Unmarried Individuals	$500,000
Married Filing Jointly	$1,000,000

In other words, the folks in this tax bracket are already in the 37% tax bracket and AMT is declawed all together for this group, and that's all they had set up to do and all we have left of the good old tenor is some phantom of AMT singing down there in the sewers somewhere.

If received a 1099 or letter saying that the income is subject to AMT, taxpayer income is subject to AMT.

Chapter IX: Kiddie Tax

In the past, if child's investment income was below $2,100, they would pay kiddie tax of 10% and if the income exceeded the $2,100 threshold, they would be taxed at their parent's tax bracket. Starting with 2018 returns, the parents' rate will not matter. Instead, investment earnings in excess of $2,100 will be taxed at the rates that apply to trusts and estates. Here are those rates for 2018:

➢ **Up to $2,550**	10%
➢ **$2,550 to $9,150**	24%
➢ **$9,150 to $12,500**	35%
➢ **Over $12,500**	37%

Example:

Billy (the kid) receives an income of $5,000. His parent's taxable income is $150,000. How much is the tax liability in 2017 vs. 2018?

Suggested Responses: In 2017, he would be taxed at his parent's level-- which was 25% in the tax bracket. Thus Billy's tax in 2017 would've been $5,000 x 25%=$1,250

In 2018, his parents are in the 22% tax bracket, thus his tax will be:

$5,000x 22%=$1,100.

The example shows that although the Trust rates shown above seems a bit harsh, in actuality Billy is better off with the new tax law, as it was tenderly intended. It goes without saying that "kiddie" refers to investment income of children under age 19 or, if full-time students, age 24, so if you were thinking of the real Billy the Kid, he wouldn't have qualified. (Use Form 8615)

Chapter X: Credits

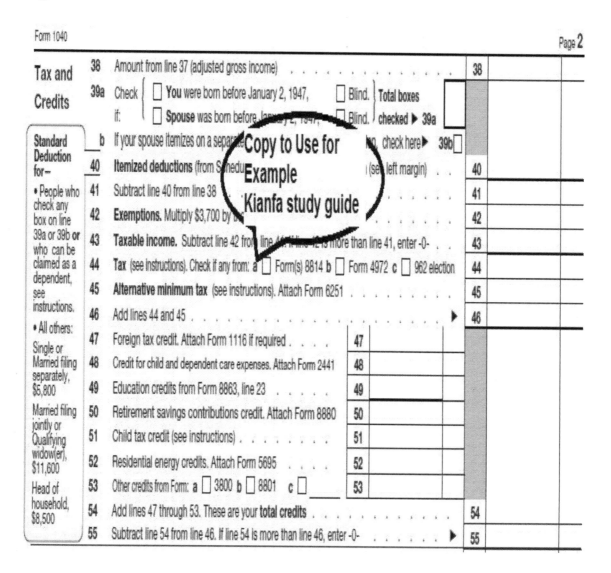

- Child and Dependent Care Credit (e.g., Form 2441 Child and Dependent Care Expenses).
- Child tax credit and additional child tax credit (e.g., Form 8812, Additional Child Tax Credit).
- Credit for Elderly and Disabled (schedule R)
- Earned Income Tax Credit (EITC) (e.g., Schedule EIC Earned Income Credit, Form 8867 Paid
- Education credits – (e.g., Form 8863 Education Credits (American Opportunity and Lifetime
- Foreign Tax Credit (form 116)

- Foreign Income (form 2555)
- Learning Credits), Form 1098T Tuition Statement).
- Preparer's Earned Income Credit Checklist).
- Retirement Savings Contribution (form 8880)

Child Tax Credit

The child tax credit is doubled for 2018 tax year (from $1,000 to $2,000), $1,400 of which will be refundable. In 2018 TCJA, there is also a $500 credit for other dependents, versus zero under current law. The lower threshold for the high-income phase-out for the Child Tax Credit changes from $110,000 AGI to $400,000 for married filers.

Prior to the TCJA, the taxpayer who was eligible to claim the child's dependent exemption was also the one eligible to claim the CTC. In turn, the taxpayer and child had to meet several "tests" for the one to be considered the dependent of the other. The TCJA eliminates the dependent exemption itself but retains the *definition* of dependent to claim the CTC as well as another child- or other dependent-related tax benefits. For Child Tax Credit reform purposes, this will usually mean that the child must be related to the taxpayer in one of several ways (son, daughter, grandchild, etc.), must live in the taxpayer's home more than half the year, and must not provide more than half of his or her own support. Special rules apply if the parents are divorced or legally separated.

All changes to the new Child Tax Credit expire after December 31, 2025.

Qualifying Child:
1. Under age 17 at the end of the tax year
2. A U.S. citizen, U.S. national, or resident of the United States
3. Claimed as your dependent
4. Your:
    a. son or daughter, an adopted child, stepchild, eligible foster child, or a descendant of any of them
    b. brother, sister, half-brother, half-sister, step-brother, step-sister, or a descendant of any of them if you care for the individual as your own child.

5. Did not provide over half of his or her own support

6. Lived with the taxpayer for more than half of the tax year

Refundable tax credits show up in the Payments and Nonrefundable tax credits show up in the Tax and Credits section of Form 1040

Examples of Refundable Credits (categorized as payments in 1040 page 2) are shown after in 1040 page 2 and categorized as "Payments"

- Estimated tax payments
- EIC
- Additional Child Tax Credit
- American Opportunity Credit (8863 line 8)
- Net Premium Credit (Form 8962)

Nonrefundable tax credits, however, show up in the <u>Tax and Credits section</u> of Form 1040. For instance, line 48-54 of 1040 in the old 1040

- Foreign tax credit
- Child and Dependent Care Credit
- Lifetime Learning Credit (line 19)
- Child Tax Credit (Became refundable from 2018-2025)
- Adoption Credit $13570 in 2017 ($13,840 for 2018)
- Savers' Credit

Earned Income Tax Credit (EITC)

This credit is for low income taxpayers whose income is often below the poverty line or they have children. Although Child Tax Credit helps, this extra credit is available based on the schedule below. The credit will first lower the liability, if any, and then provide a refund for the tax payer. This year TCJA has taken the front burner, but the PATH Act (of 2015) is still simmering on the backburner and still is in effect. The PATH Act made the following changes that will affect individuals who claim EITC on their returns:

- Individuals cannot file an amended return to claim EITC for prior years that a qualifying child did not have a Social Security Number. This provision went into effect on the date the PATH Act became law on December 18, 2015.
- The IRS can bar an individual from claiming EITC for 10 years if the IRS finds they have fraudulently claimed the credit.
- The EITC is now subject to the penalty for an erroneous claim for refunds and credits.
- Incorrectly claimed refundable credits will now be taken into account when determining the underpayment penalty.
- All other information relating to EITC remains intact (qualified Dependent: relationship, age, income, residency)

The penalty for failure to comply with the due-diligence requirements is $500 for each failure, which is adjusted for inflation (Sec. 6695(g)). Under the due-diligence regulations, the $520 penalty on preparers for each breach of the rules applies separately to each credit, meaning a preparer could conceivably be subject to as many as three penalties for one tax return for failing to exercise due diligence for the child tax credit, the American opportunity tax credit, and the EITC. For 2018, the inflation-adjusted penalty is $520.

 Earned Income Credit

Remember, this really needs your due diligence since it is 4 out of 5 mistakes by tax preparers happen here. You are eligible to receive the EIC if:

- No EIC if the person has disqualified income of over $3,400
- No one else can claim them.
- If child is married, may not qualify.

Disqualifiers are: interest, dividends income, royalty, net rent, net capital gain income, and net passive income.

2018 Earned Income Tax Credit

Income Qualification Item	No Children	With 1 Child	With 2 Children	With 3+ Children
1. Max. 2017 Earned Income Tax Credit Amount	$520	$3,468	$5,728	$6,444
2. Earned Income (lower limit) required to get maximum credit	$6,800	$10,200	$14,320	$14,320
3. Phaseout Threshold Amount Begins **(for Single, SS, or Head of Household)**	$8,510	$18,700	$18,700	$18,700
4. Phaseout Amount When Credit Ends **(for Single, SS, or Head of Household)**	$15,310	$40,402	$45,898	$49.298
5. Phaseout Threshold Amount Begins **(for Married Filing Jointly)**	$14,200	$24,400	$24,400	$24,400
6. Phaseout Amount When Credit Ends **(for Married Filing Jointly)**	$21,000	$46,102	$51,598	$54,998

Investment income must be $3,500 or less for the year to qualify for the EITC.

You must have "**earned" the income** from employment, self-employment or another source and meet certain rules.

- Form 8862
- If you are married, you must file jointly to claim this.
- The qualifying child (living 6 mos. out of the year) or permanently and totally disabled

Education Credit

No matter which of the two education credits you qualify for – the American Opportunity Tax Credit or the Lifetime Learning Tax Credit – they both operate from the same principle. The tuition and fees deduction are subtracted from your gross income (To reduce your AGI). Your tax will be lower. It's often better to use a tax credit than a deduction. Often you will receive a 1098-T to show the amount paid to the education institute which will be the amount to use as Education Credit.

If a taxpayer receives a 1098 E, chances are they must have been graduated while back and they are paying the Education Tuition or Interest which will be used in AGI to reduce the liability not to generate a refundable credit as AOA and Lifetime Learning is used.

A student enrolled in an eligible educational institution who is either: you or your spouse, your dependent for whom you claim exemption. Eligible educational institutions are Colleges and universities--and some vocational schools but do not include correspondence schools. If the taxpayers are a full-time student at the accredited college for at least 5 months of the year, they will receive a 1098-T, which shows how much they have expended during the tax year.

- Tuition and fees required for enrollment or attendance at an eligible postsecondary educational institution, but not including personal, living or family expenses, such as room and board. Up to $4,000 of college tuition if your MAGI does not exceed $65,000 (single) and $2,000 if above $65,000.
- The American Opportunity credit is a maximum annual credit of $2,500 per student.
- The Tuition and Fees deduction is a maximum of $4,000.
  (https://www.irs.gov/publications/p970/ch06.html)

- The Student Loan Interest deduction is $2,500 of qualified loan interest paid

- You can reduce your income subject to tax by up to $4,000.

The **American Opportunity Credit/Hope Credi**t is for undergraduate studies only, Use form 8863 to claim up to $2,500. The AOC is Refundable Credit which means it can give you a Tax Refund.

The **Lifetime Learning Credit** is up to a maximum of $2,000 per return and goes beyond Bachelor degree.

The **Lifetime Learning Credit** or the **Tuition and Fees Deduction,** you cannot take both in the same year. The LLC is a Nonrefundable Credit, which means, although it reduces your tax liability, it will not yield a refund check for the taxpayer.

The credit is a dollar-for-dollar reduction for tax owed, while the deduction is used to reduce the amount of income subject to tax.

If you already have a college degree and want to continue your education, then you have a choice when it comes to the form of your education tax break. You can either go for the Lifetime Learning Tax Credit, or take a deduction. The math problem is: when is it better for you to take the deduction?

The Lifetime Learning Tax Credit is a more powerful tax break. First, it is a credit, meaning that the money you receive is subtracted from your total tax obligation. Therefore, if you receive a $2,000 credit, your taxes are reduced by $2,000. That is stronger than a deduction, which reduces your taxable income. The total possible education deduction is $4,000. Your actual savings from taking the full deduction would be:

$4,000 x Effective Tax Rate=Tax Break

Limit on modified adjusted gross income (MAGI):

$160,000 if married filing joint return; $80,000 if single, head of household, or qualifying widow(er).

In Short: Qualified Scholarship for a degree program is nontaxable, but Education credits for AOA and Lifetime Learning are limited in an amount per year:

- **AOA:** up to $2,500 per student for first four years of higher education tuition paid. The first 2,000 expenses are credited 100% and anything spent beyond that will yield 25% of the expenses. For instance if a taxpayer spent $3,000, the first $2,000 + (25% of 1,000) $250=$2,250 credit.
- **Lifetime Learning Credits** Up to 20% of tuition paid (maximum credit is $2,000);

See the next page for a short table of income limits to qualify for the Education Credit.

THRESHOLD FOR EDUCATION CREDITS		
	AOA EDUCATION CREDIT	LIFETIME
MFJ	$160,000–$180,000	$110,000- $130,000
SINGLE	$80,000–$90,000	$ 55,000-$65,000

Additional Child Tax Credit: General Eligibility

The child tax credit is generally a nonrefundable credit; however, certain taxpayers may be entitled to a refundable additional child tax credit.

- Taxpayers with more than $3,000 of taxable earned income may be eligible for the additional child tax credit regardless of the number of qualifying children
- Taxpayers with three or more children may also be eligible for additional child tax credit regardless of their income
- Form 8812 is used to calculate the allowable additional child tax credit

See Tab A, Exemption, and the worksheet in the instruction booklets for additional information (including definitions and special rules relating to an adopted child, foster child, or qualifying child of more than one person).

$500 Nonrefundable Credit for Dependents

The tax reform bill also includes a nonrefundable $500 "family credit" for other dependents. The TCJA allows a new $500 nonrefundable credit for dependents who do not qualify for the child tax credit. Taxpayers can claim this credit for children who are too old for the child tax credit, as well as for non-child dependents.   Examples might include an aging parent who depends on you for care or a child whose support you provide but is 17 years old or older.

There is no SSN requirement to claim this credit, so taxpayers can claim the credit for children with an Individual Tax Identification Number (**ITIN**) or an Adoption Tax Identification Number (ATIN) if they otherwise qualify.

Taxpayers cannot claim the credit for themselves or their spouse (if MFJ).

In 2026, the credit for non-child dependents will no longer be available.

Other Credits

1. Adoption Credit ($13,840 for 2018, but it was $13,570 in 2017)
2. Health coverage credit
3. Energy credit
4. First time homebuyer
5. Dependent Care Credit

Adoption Credit

For 2018, the maximum adoption credit or exclusion for employer-provided adoption benefits has increased to $13,840. In order to claim either the credit or exclusion, your modified AGI must be less than $247,580.

Other credits such as Energy Credit and First Time homebuyer deal with the previously applied credits and expired now. They are still in the 1040 but may go away in a couple of years.

Dependent Care Credit

The limit for this credit is $3,000 for one dependent and $6,000 for two or more even if you spent more, deduct all tax-free benefits received from the employer.

Who is the Qualifying Dependent?

- Your dependent qualifying child who is under age 13 when the care is provided,

- Your spouse who is physically or mentally incapable of self-care and lived with you for more than half of the year, or

- An individual who is physically or mentally incapable of self-care, lived with you for more than half of the year, and either: (i) is your dependent; or (ii) could have been your dependent except that he or she has gross income that equals or exceeds the exemption amount, or files a joint return, or you (or your spouse, if filing jointly) could have been claimed as a dependent on another taxpayer's 2017 return.

Credit percentage is 20%-30% up to $3,000- for one child and $6,000 for 2 and more. For AGI under $15,000 the percentage is 35% **[the higher AGI the lower the percentage. Say, $40,000 AGI credits 22%]**

Keep in mind that this $3,000 or $6,000 is not the amount of credit, but the basis for calculation of credit. For instance, if a Married couple have three children in a daycare and paid $7,000 and their AGI is 34,000 (which is they are at a 25% rate) their Dependent care credit is

- Maximum Credit for three children is $6,000 (because the credit as mentioned is maxed out at $6,000.
- They are at 25% bracket, so 6,000 x .25=$1,500

Thus, the couple who paid $7,000 for daycare will receive 1,500 credits which is claimed on form 2441. If the employer funded the childcare, then that amount should be taken into consideration.

Employment Taxes for Household Employers (Nanny Tax)

If you pay someone to come to your home and care for your dependent or spouse, you may be a household employer. If you are a household employer, you will need an employer identification number (EIN) and you may have to pay employment taxes. If the individuals who work in your home are self-employed, you are not liable for any of the taxes discussed in this section. Self-employed persons who are in business for themselves are not household employees. Usually, you are not a household employer if the person who cares for your dependent or spouse does so at his or her home or place of business.

If you have a household employee, you may be subject to:

1. Social security and Medicare taxes,
2. Federal unemployment tax, and
3. Federal income tax withholding.

Related Parties

- Members of immediate family
- An individual and a corporation in which he or she owns more than 50%. Two corporations that are members of a controlled group—they have certain owners in common

Chapter XI: Accounting Methods

Cash Method

Records revenues when cash is received and expenses when cash is paid. Doctors, Dentists, Speakers, DJs, Wedding planners, and many other small businesses use Cash Basis accounting.

- Income and expenses are reported when cash is exchanged.
- It's the easiest form, but...
- Mostly for service industry—no inventory to produce income unless you qualify for small business exception, such as PSC, or your average income for the last three years is below 10 million.
- Income can be in-kind,
- Exceptions: Corporations (other than S) cannot use Cash bases. Likewise, Partnerships that have a corporation as a partner. Corporations with over 10 million sales cannot use cash basis.

<u>Think about this:</u>

In Cash basis, you will records revenues when cash is received and expenses when cash is paid.   What will happen if you paid for insurance for a year ahead?

There's a principle in Bookkeeping that records everything based on **historical cost.**

For instance if you purchased a land 20 years ago for $10,000, how much do you think this land is posted in your books?

If you use this method, report all items of income in the year in which you actually or constructively receive them. Generally, you deduct all expenses in the year you actually pay them. This is the method most individual taxpayers use.

- ➤ ***Constructive receipt.*** Generally, you constructively receive income when it is credited to your account or set apart in any way that makes it available to you. You do not need to have physical possession of it. For example, interest credited to your bank account on December 31, 2011, is taxable income to you in 2011 if you could have withdrawn it in 2011 (even if the amount is not entered in your passbook or withdrawn until 2012).

- ➤ ***Garnished wages.*** If your employer uses your wages to pay your debts, or if your wages are attached or garnisheed, the full amount is constructively received by you. You must include these wages in income for the year you would have received them.

- ➢ **Debts paid for you.** If another person cancels or pays your debts (but not as a gift or loan), you have constructively received the amount and generally must include it in your gross income for the year.

- ➢ **Payment to third party.** If a third party is paid income from property you own, you have constructively received the income. It is the same as if you had actually received the income and paid it to the third party.

- ➢ **Payment to an agent.** Income an agent receives for you is income you constructively received in the year the agent receives it. If you indicate in a contract that your income is to be paid to another person, you must include the amount in your gross income when the other person receives it.

- ➢ **Check received or available.** A valid check that was made available to you before the end of the tax year is constructively received by you in that year. A check that was "made available to you" includes a check you have already received, but not cashed or deposited. It also includes, for example, your last paycheck of the year that your employer made available for you to pick up at the office before the end of the year. It is constructively received by you in that year whether or not you pick it up before the end of the year or wait to receive it by mail after the end of the year.

- ➢ **No constructive receipt.** There may be facts to show that you did not constructively receive income.

Accrual method

If one is engaged in Income from Self Employment, LLC, Partnership or S corporation, he or she may record revenues when they are earned and expenses when they are incurred, regardless of the timing of cash receipts or payments

Under the accrual basis of accounting, expenses are matched with revenues on the income statement when the expenses incur, rather than at the time when expenses are paid. The balance sheet is also affected at the time to show increase in Accounts Payable, or a decrease in Prepaid Expenses (if the expense was paid in advance).
A good criterion for Accrual Accounting is to determine at what point the Revenue is construed as accrued and when expenses are accrued and have to be paid. Here are some criteria:

1. Delivery has occurred or services have been rendered

2. There is a persuasive evidence of an arrangement for customer payment

3. The price is fixed or determined

4. Collection is reasonably assured

Companies that deals with products (and keep inventory) use this method, but many other companies can benefit from the Accrual method as well. In short:

- It's preferable under GAAP
- If you estimated a gross income at the end of the year and next year you found it to be different, adjust it for the next year's income.
- If income is more than $5 million.
- If advance payment for the future year service, then only income what is this year's income.
- If your income is made out of services and goods, you need to treat them as two agreements.
  - Exceptions: Related parties (family or business 50%) cannot use accrual.

Chapter XII Healthcare Issues-- Individuals and Small Businesses

The Affordable Care Act (ACA) provisions

What are two ways to make the Affordable Care Act, unaffordable again? By eliminating the individual mandate-- and then limiting the responsibility of businesses to do their share at the same time. By reducing the amount of penalty for those who go without health insurance, the individual mandate to zero, TCJA hopes to upend the healthcare plan.

Here are some of the final components of the new tax law that will affect benefits and medical expenses:

Benefits-Related Provisions	H.R.1 (115) – Tax Reform Law
ACA Individual Mandate	Reduces penalty for not carrying minimum essential coverage to $0, beginning January 2019
Medical Expense Deduction	Deduction allowed for non-reimbursed qualified medical expenses exceeding 7.5% of adjusted gross income for tax years 2017 and 2018 (applies to taxpayers or spouses who are 65 or older for tax years 2012-2016)
Paid Family Leave	Creates a temporary tax credit for employers who provide paid family and medical leave to employees Business tax credit is equal to 12.5% - 25% of the wages they pay to certain employees on qualified family and medical leave Employers must: Pay at least 50% of hourly pay rate (or a prorated amount for non-hourly paid employees) for employees on leave AND Provide at least two weeks of paid leave per year The amount of the credit increases by .25% for every percent above the 50% rate of pay capping at 25% for leave pay equaling 100% of pay Applies to tax years 2018 and 2019.

TCJA requirement for Shared Responsibility payment

According to the March 19, 2018 IRS post, the "individual shared responsibility provision" requires taxpayers or required them, to do at least one of the following:

- Have qualifying health coverage called minimum essential coverage

- Qualify for a health coverage exemption

- Make a shared responsibility payment with their federal income tax return for the months that without coverage or an exemption.

Under the recently enacted Tax Cuts and Jobs Act, taxpayers must continue to report coverage, qualify for an exemption, or pay the individual shared responsibility payment for tax years 2017 and 2018.

Minimum essential coverage includes:

- Most health coverage provided by your employer

- Health insurance purchased through a Health Insurance Marketplace in the area where you live, where you may qualify for financial assistance

- Coverage provided under a government-sponsored program for which you are eligible - including Medicare, most Medicaid, and health care programs for veterans

- Health insurance purchased directly from an insurance company

- Other health coverage that is recognized by the Department of Health & Human Services as minimum essential coverage.

Individual Mandate *Penalty* - eliminated for 2019

As discussed earlier, for tax years 2016, 2017, and 2018, the healthcare tax penalty is the greater of $695 per individual (up to a maximum of $2,085) or 2.5% of household income, less the taxpayer's filing threshold amount. The Tax Cuts and Jobs Act of 2017 (TCJA) eliminates the Affordable Care Act penalty beginning in tax year 2019. Because the TCJA makes other changes that interact with how the ACA penalty is calculated, taxpayers who expect to pay a penalty in 2017 and 2018 should be aware of the other changes as they estimate their tax liability.

Changes in employee fringe benefits

The new tax reform legislation includes important changes to the tax treatment of family paid medical leave as mentioned earlier as well as other employer sponsored benefits program such as transportation benefit and moving expense reimbursements. **Here are some of the changes:**

- **Qualified Transportation Fringe Benefits and Unrelated Business Income**

The big bill swallows the tax benefits of employer-sponsored transportation or parking costs though it preserves the employer's deduction for travel expenses as well as costs associated with the employee's safety.

If some companies had a pre-tax transportation fringe benefits program, that program is not a qualified pre tax expense for the employees and businesses (particularly exempt organizations) can no longer offer pre-tax benefits to employees whose expenses may deem Unrelated Business Taxable Income (UBTI). We are now counting on churches to come out and fight this with the support of some higher authority than the US government, otherwise hope that the IRS will issue further guidance on this issue very soon. Nevertheless, for now the arrows have been released and are carried by wind to where you are.

Section V: PRACTICE AND PROCEDURES

Chapter XIII: The Tax Preparer's Sphinx

IRS encourages everyone to E-File and has partnered with software providers to make it easy, safe, and quick for anyone whose adjusted gross income (AGI) is $60,000 or less.

Volunteers are available in communities nationwide providing free tax assistance to low and moderate income. At selected sites, taxpayers can input and electronically file their own tax return with the assistance from an IRS-certified volunteer.

A tax professional is required by law to notify a taxpayer of an error on his or her tax return. A tax professional is also required by law to notify the taxpayer of the consequences of *not* correcting the error. However, a tax professional is not required to actually correct the error.

 Example:

Terrence Jones is a taxpayer who goes to Janice Smith, who is an Enrolled Agent (EA), in order to prepare his tax returns. Terrence is a new client who has always prepared his own tax returns. When Terrence makes his tax interview appointment, Janice tells him to bring his prior year return. When Terrence arrives for his appointment, Janice notices that Terrence made a large error on his prior-year, self-prepared tax return when calculating his Mortgage Interest Deduction.

Janice is required to notify Terrence of the error, as well as the consequences of not correcting the error. She encourages Terrence to file an amended tax return in order to correct the mistake. Terrence declines because he does not want to pay for an amended tax return for the prior year. Janice notes in her work papers that Terrence has declined to amend his return, even though she has warned him of the consequences. Janice has therefore fulfilled her professional obligation to notify the taxpayer of the prior year error.

***Special Note*: The U.S. Internal Revenue Code makes it a federal crime for tax professionals who "knowingly or recklessly" disclose confidential taxpayer information to third parties or who use such information for any non-preparation purpose. This is a federal misdemeanor punishable by a fine of $1,000 and prison of up to one year.

A tax preparer is required to determine a taxpayer's residency. In other words, the preparer must determine whether or not the taxpayer is considered a *resident* or *nonresident*. The rules for determining residency for tax purposes are completely different than what is established under current immigration law. A person who has a "green card" or a "student visa" may still be considered a resident of the United States for tax purposes, even if he or she does not have a Social Security Number.

A Social Security Number is required for the taxpayer, the taxpayer's spouse (if married), and any dependent listed on the tax return. A nonresident alien who is not eligible for a Social Security Number must request an Individual Taxpayer Identification Number. The issuance of an ITIN does not:

- Entitle the recipient to Social Security benefits or the Earned Income Tax Credit
- Create a presumption regarding the individual's immigration status
- Give the individual the right to work in the United States

Taxpayers who cannot obtain an SSN must apply for an ITIN if they file a U.S. tax return or are listed on a tax return as a spouse or dependent. These taxpayers must file **Form W-7**, *Application for Individual Taxpayer Identification Number*, and supply documentation that will establish foreign status and true identity. A federal tax return must generally be filed along with **Form W-7**.

 Example:
Kamala is a U.S. citizen and has a Social Security Number. In January 2010, Kamala marries José Martinez, a citizen of Mexico. José has one child from a prior marriage named Graciela. Kamala decides to file jointly with Jose in 2010, and also claim her step-daughter, Graciela, as a dependent. In order to file jointly and claim the child, they must request ITINs for José and Graciela. They must file **Form W-7**, *Application for Individual Taxpayer Identification Number*, and supply the required documentation.

Adopted children may be claimed as dependents even if they do not have a Social Security Number yet. If the taxpayer is unable to secure a Social Security Number for a child until the adoption is final, he may request an Adoption Taxpayer Identification Number (ATIN).

The ATIN may NOT be used in order to claim the Earned Income Credit. A taxpayer should apply for an ATIN only if he or she is adopting a child *and* meets all of the following qualifications:

- The child is legally placed in the taxpayer's home for legal adoption.
- The adoption is a domestic adoption OR the adoption is a legal foreign adoption and the child has a Permanent Resident Alien Card or Certificate of Citizenship.
- The taxpayer cannot obtain the child's existing SSN even though she has made a reasonable attempt to obtain it from the birth parents, the placement agency, and other persons.
- The taxpayer cannot obtain an SSN for the child from the Social Security Administration for any reason (for example, the adoption is not final).
- Administration for any reason (for example, the adoption is not final).

An ATIN can be requested for an adopted child using IRS **Form W-7A,** *Application for Taxpayer Identification Number for Pending U.S. Adoptions*. Generally, anyone who files a tax return or claims a dependent must have a Taxpayer Identification Number: either an ITIN, ATIN, or an SSN.

***Exception*: A Child Who Is Born and Dies in the Same Tax Year

1. Penalties to be assessed by the IRS against a preparer for negligent or intentional disregard of rules and regulations, and for a willful understatement of liability (e.g., IRC 6694(a), IRC 6694(b)).
2. Appropriate use of Form 8867 Paid Preparer's Earned Income Credit Checklist and related penalty for failure to exercise due diligence (e.g., IRC 6695(g)).
3. Furnishing a copy of a return to a taxpayer (e.g., IRC 6695(a)).
4. Signing returns and furnishing identifying (PTIN) numbers (e.g., IRC 6695(b), IRC 6695(c)).
5. Rules for the return preparer for keeping copies and/or lists of returns prepared (e.g., IRC 6695(d)).
6. Compliance with e-file procedures (e.g., timing of taxpayer signature, timing of filing, recordkeeping, prohibited filing with pay stub).
7. Completion and use of Form 2848 Power of Attorney and Declaration of Representative and Form 8821 Tax Information Authorization.
8. Safeguarding taxpayer information (e.g., Publication 4600 Safeguarding Taxpayer Information, Quick Reference Guide for Business, IRC 7216).

Circular 230 Subparts A, B, and C (excluding D, E), but not limited to the following:

Preparer's due diligence for accuracy of representations made to clients and IRS; reliance on third-party work products.

SELF-DISCLOSURE SUBJECT TO VERIFICATION. When applying for a PTIN, paid preparers are asked to self-disclose if they are compliant with their personal and business taxes, under penalty of perjury. Automated tax compliance checks will be performed on all paid preparers. Paid preparers are also asked if they have been convicted of a felony in the past 10 years, under penalty of perjury. The PTIN application includes space to write an explanation for both tax compliance and felony information.

The Florida Keys
Key West
Close To Perfect - Far From Normal

The Internal Revenue Service e-*file* Program allows taxpayers to schedule the payment for withdrawal on a future date. Scheduled payments must be effective on or before the return due date. As an example, a Provider may transmit an individual income tax return in February and the taxpayer can specify that the withdrawal be made in April as long as it is on or before the return due date.

As of 2017, the IRS had issued approximately 110,000 PTINs, approximately 60 percent of which were issued to paid preparers with existing PTINs and approximately 40 percent of which were issued to paid preparers without existing PTINs.

APPLYING PROPOSED CHANGES TO CIRCULAR 230. A competency test will be required (with exceptions noted) to become an officially registered tax return preparer.

- Paid preparers who have a valid PTIN before competency testing is available will have until 2013 to pass a competency test.

- Paid preparers who register for a PTIN after testing is available must pass a competency test before obtaining a PTIN.

- IRS plans to develop and implement one competency test for individuals who prepare returns from the individual tax return (Form 1040) series and will assess whether IRS needs to add additional tests in the future. Enrolled actuaries and enrolled retirement plan agents will be exempt from the paid preparer competency testing requirement if they only prepare tax returns within their limited practice areas, and will be exempt from the continuing education requirement.

- Competency tests will also be available at national and international locations.

- The test will allow individuals to consult forms and instructions during the test.

- A fee will be charged each time the candidate takes the test.

Per the IRS, registrants who provide false information on their PTIN applications will have severely limited appeal rights if IRS proposes to deny them their PTINs.

As of early July 2011, the IRS had issued approximately 730,000 PTINs, approximately 60 percent of which were issued to paid preparers with existing PTINs and approximately 40 percent of which were issued to paid preparers without existing PTINs.

 Example:

As tax preparer if you noticed some errors on last year's filing, what are your best options?

A.   Let the Taxpayer know and recommend amendment
B.   Make the necessary correction and amend with 1040X
C.   If the client did not want to amend, report the discrepancy to IRS
D.   Just jot down your note to the customer and keep in your file.

Solution:
The correct answer is D. You need to notify them, but the choice is theirs. If they chose not to amend, note this and keep your finding and recommendation in your own file.

To be able to practice before the IRS you must be an Enrolled Agent, Enrolled Actuary, and Attorney or a CPA. You may have a limited representation on practice by a AFSP participant.

The Violations You Can Avoid

As a registered Tax preparer, you need to be aware of requirement to furnish information to IRS upon request and make sure of prompt disposition of matters before the IRS.

➢ The U.S. Internal Revenue Code makes it a federal crime for tax professionals who "knowingly or recklessly" disclose confidential taxpayer information to third parties or who use such information for any non-preparation purpose. This is a federal misdemeanor punishable by a fine of $1,000 and prison of up to one year. Exceptions apply for disclosures mandated by law or a court or for disclosure for use in preparing state or local tax returns. Generally, in order for the criminal penalties to apply, criminal intent must be proven. Ordinary preparer negligence does not qualify as "criminal intent." This law became effective in 1997

➢ A registered tax preparer (prior to 2011) and AFSP participants (Currently) may not seek assistance of a CPA, an attorney, or an EA who is prohibited by the IRS, or otherwise disbarred.

Rules regarding fees, including contingent fees:

 Example:

You can charge your clients based on various systems you structure EXCEPT
A.   the number of forms and schedules you file on their behalf
B.   The amount of time you take to file their return
C.   The amount of refund you can manage to get for them.
D.   Standard of business practice.

Review Circular 230 for dealing with clients, including return of client records, conflicts of interest, advising on omissions and errors, solicitation (including advertising), and negotiation of taxpayer refund checks.

 Example:

Client is being audited and asks you to return to him/her all the records he/she furnished to you. Since you need those records in case you are audited, you refuse. You are in violation of Circular 230.

- Those AFSP participants who constantly show Incompetence or engage in disreputable conduct can face disciplinary proceedings.

- The only IRS insignia that can be used by Tax preparer is the IRS e-file logo in their advertising material.

 Example:

You just passed the AFSP/AFTR Test, you cannot advertise as: "We work closely with IRS," or "Tax Agent certified by IRS, or even "Certified by IRS,"

Response:

No way, Mr. Jones. Just say you are an AFSP participant.

Chapter XIV: Due Diligence

A tax professional is required, by law, to notify a taxpayer of an error on his or her tax return. A tax professional is also required by law to notify the taxpayer of the consequences of *not* correcting the error. However, a tax professional is not required to actually correct the error.

Example:

The taxpayer tells you that the other Accounting firm filed her return last year and she got back $2,000 and she expects the same refund if you can do it. You need to ask to see her last year's filing papers, her W2 or 1099, and examine last year's return, apply some due diligence on this year's reported income before thinking of competition.

"Due Diligence is more than a check mark on a form or clicking through tax preparation software..."

(a) In general. A practitioner must exercise due diligence:
(1) In preparing or assisting in the preparation of, approving, and filing tax returns, documents, affidavits, and other papers relating to Internal Revenue Service matters;
(2) In determining the correctness of oral or written representations made by the practitioner to the Department of the Treasury; and
(3) In determining the correctness of oral or written representations made by the practitioner to clients with reference to any matter administered by the Internal Revenue Service.
(b) Reliance on others. Except as provided in §§ 10.34, 10.35 and 10.37, a practitioner will be presumed to have exercised due diligence for purposes of this section if the practitioner relies on the work product of another person and the practitioner used reasonable care in engaging, supervising, training, and evaluating the person, taking proper account of the nature of the relationship between the practitioner and the person.

Due Diligence promotes accurate claims. Incorrect tax returns and failure to comply with the due diligence requirements can adversely affect you and your client. A practitioner must exercise due diligence when performing the following duties.

- If you prepare a client's return and any part of an understatement of tax liability is due to an unreasonable position, the IRS can assess a minimum penalty of $1,000 (IRC § 6694(a)) against you. If the understatement is due to reckless or intentional disregard of rules or regulations, the minimum penalty is $5,000 (IRC § 6694(b)).

- You can be subject to disciplinary action by the IRS Office of Professional Responsibility.
- You and your firm can face suspension or expulsion from participation in IRS e-file.
- You can be barred from preparing tax returns.
- You can be subject to criminal prosecution.

Chapter XV: Ethics Review

1. Preparer's <u>due diligence</u> for accuracy of representations made to clients and IRS; reliance on third-party work products.

2. What constitutes practice before the IRS and categories of individuals who may practice?

3. As a Registered Tax Preparer, you can only represent your client as far as the tax you prepared.

4. You are required to furnish information to IRS upon request.

5. Prompt disposition of matters before the IRS.

6. Prohibition on receiving assistance from or providing assistance to disciplined practitioners.

7. Rules regarding fees, including contingent fees.

8. Rules in dealing with clients, including return of client records, conflicts of interest, advising on omissions and errors, solicitation (including advertising), and negotiation of taxpayer refund checks.

9. Due diligence standards with respect to tax returns and other documents; standards for signing, advising positions on returns and advising submissions of other documents; advising on penalties; good faith reliance on client information; reasonable inquiries regarding incomplete, inconsistent, incorrect information.

10. Responsibility of individual(s) who have principal authority over a firm's tax practices.

11. Incompetence and disreputable conduct that can result in disciplinary proceedings.

12. Sanctions that may be imposed under Circular 230.

 Example:
After assessment, as a general rule, the Internal Revenue Service has the authority to collect outstanding federal taxes for which of the following:
A. Three years.
B. Five years.
C. Ten years.
D. Twenty years.

The correct answer is C. the Internal Revenue Service has the authority to collect outstanding federal taxes for as far as 10 years back.

 Example:

Your client says she forgot to bring her IDs, or her last years return. She shows you the paystub for December 31 that shows salary and deductions for the year. She said that's all she had last year when she filed and offers extra cash if you can file for her. If she cannot come back with proper IDs or evidence of income, it's okay to lose this client.

True or False:

A federal tax lien gives the Internal Revenue Service a legal claim to your property as security for payment of your tax debt.

Answer:

True, The Internal Revenue Service may use a levy to legally seize your property to satisfy a tax debt.

Individual return is always due on April 15 unless there are national (or sometimes State) Holidays.

The following dates provided could serve as a general example. For 2019 the individual return filing date is April 15th.

For Businesses, the due date is 2 ½ months after the end of their fiscal year. For instance if the year ends in September 30, the return is due on December 15th. Thus if the calendar year is used in business, the due date will be March 15. IRS usually posts the due date each year in the irs.gov before December 31st.

Chapter XVI: Due Date to File Income Tax

When to File Your 1040

TAX FILING FORMS	FILING DEADLINE*	Late Filing Extension
Individual 1040, SCHEDULE C, SMALL BUSINESS	**April 15, 2019**	**or submit form 4868 for a free, no penalty 6 months Extension**
1065 PARTNERSHIP, LLP, LLC	March 15,2019	**Or submit Form 7004 to get an extension until Octobor 15th.**
1120S and 1120 Corporation If Calendar year is used	March 15	**Or submit Form 7004 to get an extension until** September 15th.

- These dates are not carved in the stone and each year because of certain holidays whether national or local they could go a few days beyond these deadlines but never before the deadlines.

Chapter XVII: Identity Theft
Tax-related identity theft (Publication 5199)

Sometimes your client or their dependents are victims of Identity theft. Sometimes the criminals are next door to your office or next to the client's home, and sometimes they are thousands of miles away. We have seen one parent take the child social security to one tax preparer, and the other who could rightfully claim the dependent child files later only to find out that the dependent was already claimed.

Validating Identity of Clients

To help prevent identity theft, return preparers should confirm identities and taxpayer identification numbers (TINs) of taxpayers, their spouses, dependents and EITC qualifying children contained on the returns to be prepared. TINs include Social Security Numbers (SSNs), Adopted Taxpayer Identification Numbers (ATINs), and Individual Taxpayer Identification Numbers (ITINs). The validation does not need to be just tied to paper documents but an actual interview that includes both documentary and non-documentary verification. For instance, I usually ask parents, what grade their kids are or what are their favorite subject in class. Sometimes you can ask them about the birthdays and see if they can quickly remember. I know some fathers may not be very good at these but it's good to see them feeling a bit guilty too, but if they turned pale, then you may need to verify more.

Many years ago, my credit card was stolen but thanks to the girl at the checkout counter, when the thief came to purchase a watch for himself, he was foiled. As the cashier asked the guy to spell his name as it appeared on the card. He failed of course, because my name is hard to spell (particularly for thieves). What is the takeaway here? Ask them for their name and spellings of their name and their dependents names and look at the ID. I hope they all pass the spelling bee.

To confirm identities, the preparer can request a picture ID reflecting the taxpayer's name and address and social security cards or other documents providing the TINs of all individuals to be listed on the return.

Despite common beliefs, it's not only individuals who can become victims of the identity theft but also criminals can use a companies letterhead and EIN number to bill clients or issue W-2's to their gang in order file for refund. To investigate the situation tax preparer needs a POA to discuss the matter with the IRS agent.

As a tax preparer you are perhaps the first person who notices this by noticing your filing was rejected by the Efile services showing the return had been filed previously. Often times, your client may receive a notice from the IRS that a refund check has been sent out, and they may be the victim of identity theft. A taxpayer may receive a notice from the IRS that shows a different address or an employer which the Taxpayer may not know.

You as a tax preparer may notice data breach and thus become a victim of the criminals who access your clients and may file for them at the earliest possible day of the tax season. This already has caused some tax preparers to blame the IRS for starting the season too early before everyone had received their W2 and got a chance to go to a tax preparer. Many tax professionals think that identity theft would decrease drastically if the IRS pushed the open season to the end of February instead of the end of January. This would have given 30 days or more for people to take action on their return and limit the fraudulent returns. However, if you noticed a data breach at your office you are given one day to report the issue to the IRS office.

If you noticed your client's SS has been compromised, or he/she came to your office suspecting an identity theft, you need to complete Form 14039, Identity Theft Affidavit and send it to the IRS with your client's photo ID and a statement. If the client has received a notice from the IRS, call the phone number on the letter.

If your client has been a victim of an identity theft, he or she is required to file his or her return by paper and pay taxes while the case is being handled by the IRS until the case is completely resolved. The Identity Protection Specialized Unit phone number is 1-800-908-4490.

Resources for further guidance in government webs: check FTC Complaints for general complaints, and check Identity Theft if your identity is stolen.

Chapter XVIII: Safeguarding Taxpayer Data

Safeguarding personally identifiable taxpayer information is of critical importance to retaining the confidence and trust of taxpayers. Appropriately handling information security incidents is also very important to retaining the confidence and trust of taxpayers. The Gramm-Leach-Bliley Act requires financial institutions – companies that offer consumers financial products or services like loans, financial or investment advice, or insurance – to explain their information-sharing practices to their customers and to safeguard sensitive data

An information security incident is an adverse event or threat of an event that can result in an unauthorized disclosure, misuse, modification or destruction of taxpayer information. If you believe an information security incident has occurred that affects the confidentiality, integrity or availability of taxpayer data or the ability for the taxpayer to prepare or file a return, you may need to report the incident. The following table includes examples of types of incidents.

For more information see the IRS procedures and controls described in IRS Publication 4600 "Safeguarding Taxpayer Data: A Guide for Your Business" available on the IRS website.

Incident Type	Description
Theft	Unauthorized removal of computers, data/records on computer media or paper files.
Loss/Accident	Accidental misplacement or loss of computers, data/records on computer media or paper files.
Unauthorized Access	A person or computer gains logical or physical access without permission to a network, system, application, data or other resource.
Unauthorized Disclosure/Usage	A person violates disclosure or use policies such as IRC sections 6713 & 7216. See "Laws and Regulations", for information on IRC sections 6713 & 7216.
Computer System/Network Attack	A virus, worm, Trojan horse or other code-based malicious entity infects a host and causes a problem such as disclosure of sensitive data or denial of services.

Protect Your Customer's Information

The Gramm-Leach-Bliley Act of 1999 (GLBA) outlines it relatively easy on how to protect your clients information whether you file and store paper copies or file and submit files digitally. Confidential information includes, but is not limited to, the following:

- Taxpayer Names
- Social Security Numbers
- Dates of birth
- Addresses
- Phone numbers
- Financial information such as loans and/or bank accounts
- Employer names and phone numbers
- Tax information
- Bankruptcy Information

These best practices include:

- Take responsibility yourself, or assign someone to be responsible for safeguards;
- Assess the risks to taxpayer information in your office. Make sure to include your operations, physical environment, computer systems and employees, if applicable;
- Make a list of the locations where you keep taxpayer information (computers, filing cabinets, and containers taxpayers may bring you);
- Write a plan of how to safeguard taxpayer information. Put appropriate safeguards in place;
- Use service providers who have policies to maintain an adequate level of information protection; and
- Monitor, evaluate and adjust your security program as your business or circumstances change.

To safeguard taxpayer information, determine the appropriate security controls for your environment based on the size, complexity, nature and scope of your activities. Security controls are the management, operational and technical safeguards you may use to protect the confidentiality, integrity and availability of your customers' information.

Examples of security controls include:

- Locking doors to restrict access to paper or electronic files
- Requiring passwords to restrict access to computer files
- Encrypting electronically stored taxpayer data
- Keeping a backup of electronic data for recovery purposes
- Shredding paper containing taxpayer information
- Removing sensitive or personal information before mailing items

The following are recommended actions for incident reporting:

- Individuals (e.g., employees and contractors) who detect a situation that may be an information security incident should immediately inform the individual designated by the business to be responsible for handling customer information security.
- The individual responsible for handling customer information security should gather information about the suspected incident.
- If you believe the incident compromises a person's identity or their personal or financial information, we recommend you refer to the FTC document, "Information Compromise and the Risk of Identity Theft: Guidance for Your Business". Among other things, this reference will help you determine when to notify local law enforcement, the Federal Bureau of Investigation, the U.S. Secret Service, the U.S. Postal Inspection Service, affected businesses and customers.

Resources: Form 4557, <u>Safeguarding Taxpayer's Data</u>, and Santa Barbara Bank tips at tpg.com

Chapter XIX: How to Interview Your Clients

Based on the IRS Form 13614-C and IRS Volunteer Tax preparation procedure

Step One: Cultivate a comfortable environment and put the taxpayer at ease.

- Introduce yourself; engage in small talk (discuss the weather, difficulty in locating the site, apologize if long wait, etc.).
- Explain the tax return preparation process—the interview, how the information they provide will assist you in determining whether they must file a return, their eligibility for tax credits, etc.
- Allow the taxpayers to share any expectations, needs, and/or concerns by asking whether they have questions before beginning and encouraging them to ask questions throughout the process. ·
- Be friendly and respectful and speak clearly and simply.

Step 2: Use active listening skills.

- Use nonverbal cues such as nodding, smiling appropriately, and making eye contact.
- Listen, and then respond by restating, paraphrasing, and/or encouraging further dialogue.

Step 3: Review the taxpayer's responses to the intake questions

- Verify that all questions on (Form 13614-C) have been addressed and answered correctly. If the taxpayer checked the "Unsure" box, provide clarification and update response to "Yes" or "No".
- All corrections to taxpayer's information should be annotated on the approved intake and interview sheet prior to completing the return.
- Ask probing questions to clarify issues.
- Review all the information documents presented by the taxpayer including W-2s, 1099s, 1098s, etc.
- When you start the interview, use one or two open-ended questions, for example, 'Was there anyone else who lived in your home besides the people listed on this form'; this is essential information for determining Head of Household filing status.

- If the taxpayer's return does not fall within the scope of the program, (1) courteously explain that volunteer services are limited to those who fall within the scope of the program, (2) encourage the taxpayer to use the intake sheet in working with another tax service, and (3) thank the taxpayer for coming and express regret you cannot assist them.

Step 4: Working with the taxpayer, complete the critical intake questions on

- Don't assume—use the interview tips and decision trees in Publication 4012 to confirm:
    - Marital status (filing status)
    - Number of qualifying exemptions
    - Eligibility for child tax credit
    - Eligibility for the earned income credit

Step 5: Advise the taxpayer of the next steps

Restate the return preparation process, quality review procedures, signature and recordkeeping requirements, etc. Make sure you have good contact information in case there are electronic filing issues.

What happens to taxpayers when incorrect returns are filed with the IRS?

The IRS will contact taxpayers by mail or telephonically to correct or notify them of errors or omissions on their return.

Potential impact of an inaccurate return on taxpayers:

1. Reduced refund
2. Delayed refund
3. Additional tax liabilities
4. Interest and other penalties
5. Notices from IRS for documentation to verify certain entries on their return
6. Time-off from work to gather the required documentation, residency documentation, birth certificates, social security records, etc. and meeting with the IRS
7. Months of dialogues and interactions with the IRS
8. Loss of wages (due to unplanned leave or loss of employment)

Some common errors:
1. Incorrect or missing social security numbers/ITIN
2. Incorrect tax entered based on taxable income and filing status
3. Computation errors in figuring the taxable income, withholding and estimated tax payments, Earned Income Credit, Standard Deduction for age 65 or over or blind, the taxable amount of social Security benefits, and Child and Dependent Care Credit. Also, missing or incorrect identification numbers for employers and child care providers
4. Withholding and estimated tax payments entered on the wrong line, and
5. Math errors - both addition and subtraction

Section A. Page 1 and Page 2 to be completed by Taxpayer

Thank you for allowing us to prepare your tax return. It is very important for you to provide the information on this form to help our certified volunteer preparer in completing your return. **If you have any questions, please ask.**

You will need your:
- Tax information such as Forms W-2, 1099, 1098.
- Social security cards or ITIN letters for you and all persons on your tax return.
- Proof of Identity (such as drivers license or other picture ID).

Part I. Your Personal Information

1. Your First Name	M. I.	Last Name	Are you a U.S. Citizen? ☐ Yes ☐ No
2. Spouse's First Name	M. I.	Last Name	Is spouse a U.S. Citizen? ☐ Yes ☐ No

3. Mailing Address	Apt#	City	State	Zip Code

4. Phone Primary:	Other:	E-mail

5. Your Date of Birth	6. Your Occupation	7. Are you Legally Blind ☐ Yes ☐ No
		8. Totally and Permanently Disabled ☐ Yes ☐ No
9. Spouse's Date of Birth	10. Spouse's Occupation	11. Is Spouse Legally Blind ☐ Yes ☐ No
		12. Totally and Permanently Disabled ☐ Yes ☐ No

13. Can your parents or someone else claim you or your spouse on their tax return? ☐ Yes ☐ No ☐ Unsure

14. Other than English what language is spoken in your home? _____

15. Are you or a member of your household considered disabled? ☐ Yes ☐ No

Part II. Family and Dependent Information

1. As of December 31, your filing status is
   - ☐ Single
   - ☐ Married: Did you live with your spouse during any part of the last six months of the year ☐ Yes ☐ No
   - ☐ Divorced or Legally Separated: Date of final decree or separate maintenance agreement: _____
   - ☐ Widowed: Year of spouse's death: _____

2. List the name of everyone below who lived in your home and outside your home that you supported during the year
   If additional space is needed please check here and use page 4 for additional information. ☐

Name (first, last) Do not enter your name or Spouse's name below.	Date of Birth (mm/dd/yy)	Relationship to you (e.g. son, mother, sister)	Number of months lived in your home	US Citizen or resident of the US, Canada or Mexico (yes/no)	Single as of 12/31/10 (yes/no)	Full-time student (yes/no)	Received more than $3650 in income (yes/no)
(a)	(b)	(c)	(d)	(e)	(f)	(g)	(h)

By my signature herein below, I state under penalty of perjury that the information I have provided in these pages are true and correct. If I have not supplied a original copy or receipt/proof of all incomes and expenses, I will provide to the IRS all originals or certifiable copies if requested by the IRS. I am providing this information for the purpose of filing my tax return to show a complete list of income, expenses, life events, filing status, family and dependent information (and dependent care credit), as well as applicable education credits whichever applicable.

Taxpayer (s) name _____   _____

Signature(s): _____   Date: _____

Section A. To be completed by Taxpayer (continued)

Part III. Income – Did you (or your spouse) receive: (Check Yes, No or Unsure to all questions below)

Yes	No	Unsure	
☐	☐	☐	1. Wages or Salary? (Form(s) W-2)
☐	☐	☐	2. Tip Income?
☐	☐	☐	3. Scholarships? (Forms W-2, 1098-T)
☐	☐	☐	4. Interest/Dividends from: checking/savings accounts, bonds, CDs, brokerage? (Forms 1099-INT, 1099-DIV, 1099-OID)
☐	☐	☐	5. Refund of state/local income taxes previously used as a deduction on 1040 Sch A? (Form(s) 1099-G)
☐	☐	☐	6. Alimony Income?
☐	☐	☐	7. Self-Employment Income/Loss (such as earnings from contract labor, small business)? (Form(s) 1099-MISC)
☐	☐	☐	8. Income (gain or loss) from the sale of Stocks, Bonds or Real Estate (including your home)? (Form(s) 1099-B)
☐	☐	☐	9. Disability Income (such as payments from SSA, VA, insurance, etc)? (Forms 1099-R, W-2)
☐	☐	☐	10. Distributions from Pensions, Annuities, and/or IRA? (Form(s) 1099-R)
☐	☐	☐	11. Unemployment Compensation? (Form(s) 1099-G)
☐	☐	☐	12. Social Security or Railroad Retirement Benefits? (Form(s) SSA-1099)
☐	☐	☐	13. Income (profit or loss) from Rental Property?
☐	☐	☐	14. Other Income: (gambling, lottery, prizes, awards, jury duty, etc.) Specify: _____ (Forms W-2 G, 1099-MISC)

Part IV. Expenses – In 2010 Did you (or your spouse) pay: (Check Yes, No or Unsure to all questions below)

Yes	No	Unsure	
☐	☐	☐	1. Alimony: If yes, do you have the recipient's SSN? ☐ Yes ☐ No
☐	☐	☐	2. Contributions to a retirement account? ☐ IRA ☐ Roth IRA ☐ 401K ☐ Other
☐	☐	☐	3. Educational expenses paid for yourself, spouse or dependents? (such as tuition, books, fees, etc.)
☐	☐	☐	4. Unreimbursed employee business expenses (such as mileage)?
☐	☐	☐	5. Medical expenses?
☐	☐	☐	6. Home mortgage interest?
☐	☐	☐	7. Real estate taxes for your home or personal property taxes?
☐	☐	☐	8. Charitable contributions?
☐	☐	☐	9. Child/dependent care expenses that allowed you and your spouse, to work or to look for work?

Part V. Life Events – Did you (or your spouse): (Check Yes, No or Unsure to all questions below)

Yes	No	Unsure	
☐	☐	☐	1. Have a Health Savings Account? (Forms 5498-SA, 1099-SA)
☐	☐	☐	2. Have debt from a mortgage or credit card canceled/forgiven by a commercial lender? (Form(s) 1099-C)
☐	☐	☐	3. Buy a home? If yes, closing date _____
☐	☐	☐	4. Have Earned Income Credit (EIC) disallowed in a prior year? If yes, for which tax year? _____
☐	☐	☐	5. Purchase and install energy efficient home items? (such as windows, furnace, insulation, etc.)
☐	☐	☐	6. Live in an area that was affected by a natural disaster? If yes, where? _____
☐	☐	☐	7. Receive the First Time Homebuyers Credit in previous years?
☐	☐	☐	8. Pay any student loan interest?

TAXPAYER STOP HERE!

Thank you for completing this form.

Section B. Completed by registered tax preparer

Remember: You are the link between the taxpayer's information and a correct tax return. Verify the taxpayer's information on pages 1 & 2 is complete. Any question marked "Unsure" must be discussed with the taxpayer and changed to "Yes" or "No".

Must be completed ONLY if persons are listed in Part II, Question 2.

☐ Yes ☐ No 1. Can anyone else claim any of the persons listed in Part II, Question 2, as a dependent on their return? If yes, which ones:

_____

_____

_____

☐ Yes ☐ No 2. Were any of the persons listed in Part II, Question 2, totally and permanently disabled? If yes, which ones:

_____

_____

☐ Yes ☐ No 3. Did any of the persons listed in Part II, Question 2 provide more than half of their own support? If yes, which ones:

_____

_____

_____

☐ Yes ☐ No 4. Did the taxpayer provide more than half the support
☐ N/A   for each of the persons in Part II, Question 2? If no, which ones:

_____

_____

☐ Yes ☐ No 5. Did the taxpayer pay over half the cost of maintaining a home for any of the persons in Part II, Question 2? If yes, which ones:

_____

_____

Reminder

Use Publication 17, *Your Federal Income Tax For Individuals*

Section C. Completed by a qualified reviewer

After reviewing the tax return and verifying that it reflects correct tax law application to the information provided by the taxpayer, check the final item.

1. **Sections A & B** of this form are complete.

2. **Taxpayer's Identity, Address** and **Phone Number** were verified.

3. **Names, SSN or ITINs, and dates of birth of taxpayer, spouse** and **dependents** match the supporting documents.

4. **Filing Status** is correctly determined.

5. **Personal** and **Dependency Exemptions** are entered correctly on the return.

6. All **Income** shown on source documents and noted in Section A, Part III is included on the tax return.

7. Any **Adjustments** to **Income** are correctly reported.

8. **Standard, Additional** or **Itemized Deductions** are correct.

9. All **Credits** are correctly reported.

10. Withholding shown on **Forms W-2, 1099** and **Estimated Tax Payments** are correctly reported.

11. If **Direct Deposit** or **Debit** was elected, checking/saving account and routing information match the supporting documents.

12. Reviewer Initials_____

☐ **Check if the items above have been verified to validate accuracy based on your interview with the taxpayer and a second review of their source documents.**

Based on the IRS Form 13614-C with minor changes

3

CHAPTER XX How long to keep tax records:

1. Keep records for 3 years if situations (4), (5), and (6) below do not apply to you.
2. Keep records for 3 years from the date you filed your original return or 2 years from the date you paid the tax, whichever is later, if you file a claim for credit or refund after you file your return.
3. Keep records for 7 years if you file a claim for a loss from worthless securities or bad debt deduction.
4. Keep records for 6 years if you do not report income that you should report, and it is more than 25% of the gross income shown on your return.
5. Keep records indefinitely if you do not file a return.
6. Keep records indefinitely if you file a fraudulent return.
7. Keep employment tax records for at least 4 years after the date that the tax becomes due or is paid, whichever is later.

The following questions should be applied to each record as you decide whether to keep a document or throw it away.

Are the records connected to property?

Generally, keep records relating to property until the period of limitations expires for the year in which you dispose of the property. You must keep these records to figure any depreciation, amortization, or depletion deduction and to figure the gain or loss when you sell or otherwise dispose of the property.

If you received property in a nontaxable exchange, your basis in that property is the same as the basis of the property you gave up, increased by any money you paid. You must keep the records on the old property, as well as on the new property, until the period of limitations expires for the year in which you dispose of the new property.

Section VI: Bonus Material

Questions and Answers

**For those who want to
Go on and become
Professional Tax preparers**

TESTING

Practice Questions and Analysis

Most of these questions are taken directly from the IRS website, publications, forms and instructions.

If you can do these on the first sitting, you have a great chance on passing it the first time

**Note: No need to time yourself on this portion.
Take your time and refer to analysis following the questions.**

Chapter XXI: Sample Questions in Individual Taxation

1- Ricardo and Lucy are married. Ricardo dies on December 3, 2018. Lucy has one dependent child, a 15-year-old daughter named Hannah. Lucy does not remarry. What is Lucy's filing status for 2008, 2019, 2020 and 2021?

2. Gracie's husband George died on July 20, 2018. Gracie has a dependent son who is three years old. How would she file in 2019? In 2020? Gracie got married to Bob in 2021, how can she file?

3. Kathy, divorced with no children, lived with her unemployed roommate Rosanne for the entire year. Kathy had to pay more than half of the cost of keeping up their apartment. Which filing status can Kathy use?

   A. Head of Household
   B. Married Filing Separately
   C. Single
   D. Qualifying Widow(er)

4. The two filing statuses that generally result in the lowest tax amounts are Married Filing Jointly and _____.

   A. Married Filing Separately
   B. Head of Household
   C. Qualifying Widow(er) with Dependent Child
   D. Single

5. Rachel is divorced and provided over half the cost of keeping up a home. Her five-year-old daughter Phoebe lived with her for seven months last year. Rachel allows her ex-husband Ross to claim their child Phoebe as a dependent. Which of the following statements is true?

   A. Ross may take Phoebe as his dependent and also file as Head of Household.
   B. Ross may take Phoebe as his dependent, and Rachel may still file as Head of Household.
   C. Neither parent qualifies for Head of Household filing status because Phoebe did not live with either parent for the entire year.
   D. Rachel cannot release the dependency exemption to Jim, because their daughter did not live with Ross for over six months.

6. To determine if a widowed taxpayer can use the Qualifying Widow(er) with Dependent Child status, a preparer needs to know all the following information EXCEPT _____.

A. The year the spouse died
B. If the taxpayer filed a joint return for the year the spouse died
C. Whether the taxpayer furnished more than half the cost for keeping up the main home of a qualified child
D. Whether the taxpayer remarried before the end of the tax year

7. Which dependent relative may qualify a taxpayer for Head of Household filing status?

   A. An adult stepdaughter whom the taxpayer supports, but who lives across town
   B. A family friend who lives with the taxpayer all year
   C. A father who lives in his own home and not with the taxpayer
   D. A child who lived with the taxpayer for three months of the tax year

8. Ginger Brown and Al Jolsen have a 5-year-old daughter, Amanda, but they are not married. Ginger and her daughter lived together all year. Al lived alone in his own apartment. Ginger earned $13,000 working as a clerk in a clothing store. Al earned $48,000 as an assistant manager of a hardware store. He paid over half the cost of Ginger's apartment for rent and utilities. He also gave Ginger extra money for groceries. Al does not pay any expenses or support for any other family member. All are U.S. citizens and have valid SSNs. Which of the following is true?

   A. Al may file Head of Household.
   B. Ginger may file Head of Household.
   C. Al and Ginger may file jointly.
   D. Neither may claim Head of Household filing status

9. Samantha has a 10-year-old child. She separated from her husband during the tax year. Which of the following would prevent Samantha from filing as Head of Household?

   A. Samantha has maintained a separate residence from her husband since April of the tax year.
   B. The qualifying child's principal home is now with Samantha.
   C. Samantha's parents assisted with 25% of the household costs.
   D. The child lived with Samantha beginning in mid-July of the tax year.

10. Roxanna's younger brother Sebastian is seventeen years old. Sebastian lived with friends from January through February of 2010. From March through July of 2010, he lived with Roxanna. On August 1, Sebastian moved back in with his friends, with whom he stayed for the rest of the year. Since Sebastian did not have a job, Roxanna gave him money every month. Roxanna had no other dependents.

    A. Roxanna may file as Head of Household for 2010.
    B. Roxanna may file jointly with Sebastian in 2010.
    C. Roxanna cannot file as Head of Household in 2010.

D. Sebastian may file as Head of Household in 2010.

11. The person who qualifies a taxpayer as Head of Household must be _____.

    A. A minor child
    B. A blood relative
    C. The taxpayer's dependent OR the taxpayer's qualifying child
    D. Someone who lives away from the taxpayer's main home

12. Gerald takes care of his grandson Kyle, who is 10 years old. How long must Kyle live in the taxpayer's home in order for Gerald to qualify for Head of Household status?

    A. At least three months
    B. More than half the year
    C. The entire year
    D. More than 12 months

13. What is the best filing status in 2010 for Dana? Dana's husband died in January 2010. She has one dependent son who is four years old.

    A. Married Filing Jointly
    B. Single
    C. Qualifying Widow
    D. Head of Household

14. Victor is 39 years old. He has been legally separated from his wife Janet since February 1, 2010. Their divorce was not yet final at the end of the year. They have two minor children. One child lives with Victor and the other child lives with Janet. The children have been with their respective parents from February through December of the tax year. Victor provides all of the support for the minor child living with him. Janet refuses to file jointly with Victor this year. Therefore, the most beneficial filing status that Victor qualifies for is:

    A. Married Filing Separately
    B. Single
    C. Head of Household
    D. Qualifying Widower with a Dependent Child

15. Sean is single. His mother Clara lives in an assisted living facility. Sean provides all of Clara's support. Clara died on June 1, 2010. She had no income. Which of the following is true?

    A. Sean may file as Head of Household and may also claim his mother as a dependent.
    B. Sean must file Single in 2010, and he cannot claim his mother as a dependent.

C. Sean may claim his mother as a dependent, but he cannot claim Head of Household status for 2010.

D. None of the above.

16. Regina's marriage was annulled in December 2010. She was married to her husband in 2008 and filed jointly with him in 2008 and 2009. Regina has no dependents.

A. Regina must file amended returns, claiming Single filing status for all open years affected by the annulment.

B. Regina is not required to file amended returns, and she must file Single on her 2010 tax return.

C. Regina is not required to file amended returns, and she must file Married Filing Separately on her 2010 tax return.

D. Regina is not required to file amended returns, and she must file Married Filing Jointly on her 2010 tax return.

17. **True or False.** A taxpayer may NEVER amend a joint tax return from "Married Filing Jointly" to "Married Filing Separately" after the filing deadline.

18. Lisa married Harry in 2005, and they have two dependent children. Harry died in 2008. Lisa has never remarried. Which filing status should be used in 2010?

A. Single

B. Married Filing Jointly

C. Head of Household

D. Qualifying Widow with Dependent Child

19. Helen and Troy are married and live together. Helen earned $7,000 in 2010, and Troy earned $42,000. Helen wants to file a joint return, but Troy refuses to file with Helen and instead files a separate return.

A. Helen may still file a Married Filing Joint tax return and sign Troy's name as an "absentee" spouse.

B. Helen and Troy must both file separate returns.

C. Helen may file as Single because Troy refuses to sign a joint return.

D. Helen does not have a filing requirement.

20. Dwight and Angela are married, but they choose to file separate tax returns for tax year 2010, because Dwight is being investigated by the IRS for an older tax year. Dwight and Angela file their separate tax returns on time. A few months later, after the investigation is over and Dwight is cleared of all wrongdoing, Dwight wishes to file amended returns and file jointly with his wife in order to claim the Earned Income Credit. Which of the following is TRUE?

A. Dwight is prohibited from changing his filing status in order to claim this credit.
B. Dwight and Angela may amend their separate tax returns to Married Filing Jointly in order to claim the credit.
C. Dwight may amend his tax return to joint filing status, but he may not claim the credit.
D. Angela may not file jointly with Dwight after she has already filed a separate tax return.

21. Sheena is in the process of adopting an infant boy. She qualifies to take the child as a dependent, but she cannot obtain a Social Security Number for the child yet. What can you advise Sheena to do in order to claim the child?

A. Sheena may file a tax return on paper and put "adopted" in the line for the SSN.
B. Sheena must wait until a valid Social Security Number is issued in order to claim the child.
C. Sheena may apply for an ATIN in order to claim the baby.
D. Sheena may not claim the child until the adoption is final.

22. Which of the following statements is TRUE regarding the HoH?

A. The taxpayer is considered unmarried on the first day of the year.
B. The taxpayer's spouse must live in the home during the tax year.
C. The taxpayer's dependent parent does not have to live with the taxpayer in order to qualify for Head of Household.
D. The taxpayer paid less than half of the cost of keeping up the house for the entire year.

Responses and Analysis

1. Analysis

- Lucy's filing status for 2018 is MFJ.
- Lucy can file as a Qualifying Widow in 2019 and 2020, which is a more favorable filing status than Single or Head of Household.
- In 2021, Lucy would qualify for Head of Household filing status.

2. Analysis

- Gracie files a joint return with George in 2019.
- In 2020, Gracie would file as a Qualifying Widow with Dependent Child.
- In 2021, however, Gracie remarries, so she no longer qualifies for the Qualifying Widow filing status. She must now file jointly with her new husband, or MFS.

3. The answer is C

The person who qualifies a taxpayer as Head of Household must be the taxpayer's qualifying child or a qualifying relative. However, a taxpayer cannot use Head of Household filing status simply because a qualifying relative lived with the taxpayer for the whole tax year

4. The answer is C

The Qualifying Widow(er) with Dependent Child filing status yields as low a tax amount as Married Filing Jointly.

5. The answer is B

Rachel may use Head of Household status because she is not married and she provided over half the cost of keeping up the main home of her dependent child for more than six months. However, because Rachel's ex-husband claims Phoebe as his dependent, the preparer must write Phoebe's name on line 4 of the filing status section of Form 1040 or 1040A.

6. The answer is B

The taxpayer must have been eligible to file a joint return; it does not matter if a joint return was actually filed.

7. The answer is C

A parent is the only dependent relative who does not have to live with the taxpayer in order for the taxpayer to claim Head of Household status.

8. The answer is D

- Al provided over half the cost of providing a home for Ginger and Amanda, but he cannot file Head of Household since Amanda (his child) did not live with him for over half the year.
- Ginger cannot file HOH either, because she does not provide more than one-half the cost of keeping up the home for her daughter, Amanda.
- However, either Al or Ginger may still claim Amanda as their dependent.

9. The answer is D

For Samantha to file as Head of Household, Samantha's home must have been the main home of her qualifying child for more than half the tax year

10. The answer is C

Roxanna cannot claim Head of Household status because Sebastian lived with her for only five months, which is less than half the year.

11. The answer is C

The taxpayer must claim the person as a dependent unless the noncustodial parent claims the child as a dependent. Answer A is incorrect, because a qualifying dependent does not have to be a minor in many cases. Answer B is incorrect because a qualifying dependent may be related by blood, marriage, or adoption.

12. The answer is B

The relative must have lived with the taxpayer *more than half the year* (over six months) and have been the taxpayer's dependent. The exception is that a taxpayer's *dependent parent* does not have to live with the taxpayer

13. The answer is A

If a taxpayer's spouse died during the year, the taxpayer is considered married for the whole year for filing status purposes, and may file as "MFJ." So Samantha may file a joint return with her husband in 2010, which is the year he died. (Publication 17)

14. The answer is C

Victor qualifies for Head of Household filing status. His child lived with him for more than six months. Victor may file as Head of Household because he is "considered unmarried" on the last day of the year and he paid more than half the cost of keeping up a home for the year for a qualifying child. Victor cannot file jointly with Jane, if she does not agree.

15. The answer is A

Because Sean paid more than half the cost of his mother's care in a care facility from the beginning of the year until her death, then he is entitled to claim an exemption for her, and he can also file as Head of Household (Publication 501).

16. The answer is A

Regina must file amended tax returns for 2008 and 2009. She cannot file jointly with her husband in 2010. If a couple obtains a court decree of annulment, which holds that no valid marriage ever existed, they are considered unmarried *even if* the couple filed joint returns for earlier years. A taxpayer must file amended returns (Form 1040X) claiming Single or Head of Household status for all tax years affected by the annulment that are not closed by the statute of limitations for filing a tax return. The statute of limitations generally does not expire until three years after an original return is filed (Publication 501).

17. False

There is only one exception: The personal representative for a decedent (a deceased taxpayer) can change from a joint return elected by the surviving spouse to a separate return for the decedent.

18. The answer is D

In 2010, Lisa qualifies for "Qualifying Widow with Dependent Child" filing status. Lisa and Harry qualified to file jointly in 2008, and Lisa signed the tax return as a surviving spouse. The year of death is the last year for which a taxpayer can file jointly with a deceased spouse. Then, in 2009, Lisa was eligible to file as a Qualifying Widow with Dependent Child. She would be eligible for the same filing status in 2010. This filing status yields as low a tax amount as Married Filing Jointly and is available for only two years following the year of the spouse's death. After two years, the filing status then converts to Single or Head of Household, whichever applies.

19. The answer is B

In this case, both spouses are required to file a tax return. Married couples must agree to file jointly. If one spouse does not agree to file jointly, they must file separately.

20. The answer is B

If a taxpayer files a separate return, the taxpayer may elect to amend the filing status to "Married Filing Jointly" at any time within three years from the due date of the original return. This does not include any extensions. However, the same does not hold true in reverse. Once a taxpayer files a *joint return*, the taxpayer cannot choose to file a separate return for that year after the due date of the return (with a rare exception for deceased taxpayers).

21. The answer is C

Sheena may request an ATIN and claim the child. An ATIN is an Adoption Taxpayer Identification Number issued by the IRS as a temporary taxpayer identification number for the child in a domestic adoption where the taxpayers are unable to obtain the child's Social Security Number. The ATIN is to be used by the adopting taxpayers on their federal income tax return to identify the child while final domestic adoption is pending.

22. The answer is C

Parents do not have to live with a taxpayer in order to take the dependency exemption. This is a special rule only for dependent parents. This rule also applies to parents or grandparents who are related to the taxpayer by blood, marriage, or adoption (examples include a stepmother or father-in-law). A taxpayer must pay over half of the household costs in order to qualify for this filing status.

Chapter XXII:

How to Represent Your Clients Before the IRS

The Annual Filing Season Program is intended to recognize and encourage unenrolled tax return preparers who voluntarily increase their knowledge and improve their filing season competency through continuing education (CE).

CONTINUING EDUCATION REQUIREMENT. IRS encourages tax preparers to take 18 hours of continuing education to stay on its database.

The 18 hours credits must be in the following categories:

10 hours – Federal Tax Law

6 hours – Annual Federal Tax Refresher

2 hours – Ethics

The following categories need 15 hours annually:

Anyone who passed the Registered Tax Return Preparer test administered by the IRS between November 2011 and January 2013.

SEE Part I Test-Passers: Tax practitioners who have passed the Special Enrollment Exam Part I within the past two years.

VITA volunteers: Quality reviewers, instructors, and return preparers.

Other accredited tax-focused credential-holders:The Accreditation Council for Accountancy and Taxation's Accredited Business Accountant/Advisor (ABA) and Accredited Tax Preparer (ATP) programs.

For those who are required to obtain 15 hours, the courses must be in the following categories:

10 hours – Federal Tax Law

3 hours – Federal Tax Law Updates

2 hours – Ethics

To be able to practice before the IRS you must be an Enrolled Agent, Enrolled Actuary, and Attorney or a CPA. You may have a limited representation rights to practice if you meet certain criteria.

In order to get the due credit, in addition to the completion of CE credits and the three-hour testing on the new tax updates (TCJA), a professional needs to make sure about the following two steps:

- Have an active <u>preparer tax identification number (PTIN)</u>.

- Consent to adhere to specific practice obligations outlined in Subpart B and section 10.51 of <u>Treasury Department Circular No. 230</u>.

In particular, learn about Subpart B and Section 10.51 shown below.

Duties and restrictions in subpart B Circ. 230

The AFSP is required consent to abide by regulations in Circular 230 SUBPART C which emphasizes on competence to practice before the IRS. Here is a refresher on 10.51.

§ 10.51 Incompetence and disreputable conduct.

1. *Incompetence and disreputable conduct.*
2. Conviction of any criminal offense involving dishonesty or breach of trust.
3. Conviction of any felony under Federal or State law.
4. Giving false or misleading information to the Department of the Treasury.
5. Solicitation of employment as prohibited under §10.30, the use of false or misleading representations with intent to deceive a client or prospective client in order to procure employment, or intimating that the practitioner is able improperly to obtain special consideration or action from the Internal Revenue Service or any officer or employee thereof.
6. Willfully failing to make a Federal tax return in violation of the Federal tax laws, or willfully evading, attempting to evade, or participating in any way in evading or attempting to evade any assessment or payment of any Federal tax.
7. Willfully assisting, counseling, encouraging a client or prospective client in violating, or suggesting to a client or prospective client to violate, any Federal tax law, or knowingly counseling or suggesting to a client or

prospective client an illegal plan to evade Federal taxes or payment thereof.

8. Misappropriation of, or failure properly or promptly to remit, funds received from a client for the purpose of payment of taxes or other obligations due the United States.

9. Directly or indirectly attempting to influence, or offering or agreeing to attempt to influence, the official action of any officer or employee of the Internal Revenue Service.

10. Disbarment or suspension from practice as an attorney, certified public accountant, public accountant, or actuary by any duly constituted authority of any State, territory, or possession of the United States, including a Commonwealth, or the District of Columbia, any Federal court of record or any Federal agency, body or board.

11. Knowingly aiding and abetting another person to practice before the Internal Revenue Service during a period of suspension, disbarment or ineligibility of such other person.

12. Contemptuous conduct in connection with practice before the Internal Revenue Service, including the use of abusive language, making false accusations or statements, knowing them to be false, or circulating or publishing malicious or libelous matter.

13. Giving a false opinion, knowingly, recklessly, or through gross incompetence, including an opinion which is intentionally or recklessly misleading, or engaging in a pattern of providing incompetent opinions on questions arising under the Federal tax laws. False opinions described in this paragraph (a)(13) include those which reflect or result from a knowing misstatement of fact or law, from an assertion of a position known to be unwarranted under existing law, from counseling or assisting in conduct known to be illegal or fraudulent, from concealing matters required by law to be revealed, or from consciously disregarding information indicating that material facts expressed in the opinion or offering material are false or misleading. For purposes of this paragraph (a)(13), reckless conduct is a highly unreasonable omission or misrepresentation involving an extreme departure from the standards of ordinary care that a practitioner should

observe under the circumstances. A pattern of conduct is a factor that will be taken into account in determining whether a practitioner acted knowingly, recklessly, or through gross incompetence.

(14)   Willfully failing to sign a tax return.

Limited Representation Rights

To summarize the tax preparers with Limited Representation Rights keep the following in mind (more details in the Q&A that will follow) :

- "A return preparer who is not an attorney, CPA, or enrolled agent and who does not participate in the Annual Filing Season Program will only be permitted to prepare tax returns. "

- "The return preparer will not be permitted to represent clients before the IRS except in regard to returns prepared by the return preparer before January 1, 2016. "

- "To have limited representation rights for any return or claim for refund prepared and signed after December 31, 2015, return preparers must participate in the Annual Filing Season Program in both the year of return preparation and the year of representation.".

AFSP participants will be included in a public database of return preparers scheduled to launch on the IRS website by January 2019. The Directory of Federal Tax Return Preparers with Credentials and Select Qualifications will include the name, city, state, zip code, and credentials of all attorneys, CPAs, enrolled agents, enrolled retirement plan agents and enrolled actuaries with a valid PTIN, as well as all AFSP – Record of Completion holders.

Participants in AFSP program, who have completed the test and consented to the Circular 230 criteria outline in Subpart C 10.51, will receive Record of Completion, which differentiates them in the marketplace. This Directory will be updated every year to show the new AFSP participants.

The AFSP Record of Completion holders will have a Limited Representation Rights authorize the tax professional to represent you if, and only if, they prepared and signed the return. They can do this only before IRS revenue agents, customer service representatives and similar IRS employees. They cannot represent clients whose returns they did not prepare. They cannot represent clients regarding appeals or collection issues even if they did prepare the return in question. For returns filed after Dec. 31, 2016, the only tax return preparers with limited representation rights are Annual Filing Season Program Participants. Other tax return preparers have limited representation rights, but only for returns filed before Jan. 1, 2016.

Q & A for the AFSP Participants

HOW AND WHEN WILL I GET MY RECORD OF COMPLETION?

After PTIN renewal season begins in October 2018, a Record of Completion will be generated to you once all requirements have been met, including renewal of your PTIN for 2018 and consent to the Circular 230 obligations.

If you have an online PTIN account, you will receive an email from TaxPro_PTIN@irs.gov with instructions on how to sign the Circular 230 consent and receive your certificate in your online secure mailbox.

If you don't have an online PTIN account, you will receive a letter with instructions for completing the application process and obtaining your certificate.

The 3 hour uninterrupted test time requires a passing score of 70 points (70 out of 100 Questions) and the deadline for the test is 12/31/2018. The provider will post the PTIN for the passing candidates on IRS website but the candidates need to go to PTIN and agree with the term and conditions in the PTIN area to be eligible for listing in the IRS directory. The candidates will continue to have limited representation rights before limited offices of the IRS with respect to clients whose returns you prepare and sign until December 31, 2018.

ARE CREDENTIALED PREPARERS PRECLUDED FROM PARTICIPATING IN THE AFSP?

This program is not designed, directed or intended for credentialed preparers who already possess a much higher level of qualification. However, if an attorney, certified professional accountant, enrolled agent, enrolled retirement plan agent, or enrolled actuary seeks to participate in the program, you would be required to meet the same CE requirements as preparers in the exempt category.

WHY DO WE NEED TO COMPLETE THE AFTR Program

The AFTR Course aims to recognize the efforts of non-credentialed return preparers who aspire to a higher level of professionalism. Meet the requirements by obtaining 18 hours of continuing education, including a six hour federal tax law refresher course with test, and once all testing requirement is done, the candidate needs to consent to at their PTIN screen Adherence and consent to duties and restrictions found in subpart B and section 10.51 of Circular 230 to receive an Annual Filing Season Program – Record of Completion from the IRS.

NOTE: AFTR course and credits are not geared to Enrolled Agents, and no CE credits are offered for those professionals who can already represent clients before the IRS.

I passed the Registered Tax Return Preparer test! What about me?

Anyone who passed the Registered Tax Return Preparer test offered between November 2011 and January 2013 only needs to meet their original 15 hour continuing education requirement each year to obtain an AFSP – Record of Completion. Those who passed the RTRP test and certain other recognized national and state tests are exempt from the six hour federal tax law refresher course with test.

DO I HAVE TO GET AN ANNUAL FILING SEASON PROGRAM – RECORD OF COMPLETION?

No, it's voluntary. Anyone with a preparer tax identification number (PTIN) can prepare tax returns for compensation, but continuing education is encouraged for all tax return preparers.

WHAT ARE THE BENEFITS OF GETTING AN AFSP – RECORD OF COMPLETION?

In addition to being included in the new public directory of tax return preparers launching in January every year, the AFSP – Record of Completion differentiates you in the marketplace. The IRS launched a public education campaign encouraging taxpayers to select return preparers carefully and seek those with professional credentials or other select qualifications. This Directory will be updated every year to show the new AFSP participants.

In addition, in the past couple of years, some changes have taken place in representation rights of return preparers.

Attorneys, CPAs, and enrolled agents will continue to be the only tax professionals with unlimited representation rights, meaning they can represent their clients on any matters including audits, payment/collection issues, and appeals. They do not need to partake in the AFTR courses to receive any CE credits.

Limited representation rights authorize the tax professional to represent you if, and only if, they prepared and signed the return. They can do this only before IRS revenue agents, customer service representatives and similar IRS employees. They cannot represent clients whose returns they did not prepare. They cannot represent clients regarding appeals or collection issues even if they did prepare the return in question. For returns filed after Dec. 31, 2015, the only tax return preparers with limited representation rights are Annual Filing Season Program Participants. Other tax return preparers have limited representation rights, but only for returns filed before Jan. 1, 2016.

HOW AND WHEN WILL I GET MY RECORD OF COMPLETION?

After PTIN renewal season begins in October 2018, a Record of Completion will be generated to you once all requirements have been met, including renewal of your PTIN for 2019, and make sure to consent to the Circular 230 obligations.

If you have an online PTIN account, you will receive an email from TaxPro_PTIN@irs.gov with instructions on how to sign the Circular 230 consent and receive your certificate in your online secure mailbox.

If you don't have an online PTIN account, you will receive a letter with instructions for completing the application process and obtaining your certificate, but you need to get online, Come On!

ARE CREDENTIALED PREPARERS PRECLUDED FROM PARTICIPATING IN THE AFSP?

This program is not designed, directed or intended for credentialed preparers who already possess a much higher level of qualification. However, if an attorney, certified professional accountant, enrolled agent, enrolled retirement plan agent, or enrolled actuary seeks to participate in the program, you would be required to meet the same CE requirements as preparers in the exempt category.

THE END: PEW.....
I HOPE YOU ENJOYED THIS BOOK.

☐ If you want to take the AFSP and take a test for the new tax law, we'll offer Trump/GOP Tax Law to reemphasize some of the topics here and focus on all changes to the tax law. Check our website fkianfa.com for tax conference.

☐ If you would like to take the IRS test in AFSP to get in the IRS Directory of tax professionals, make sure to give us call 954-399-8980 to get updated material and if you like to take some face to face workshops. fkianfa@gmail.com

☐ **The Yearly Updates can be found at our website: Click on Updates at fkianfa.com for all future tax years.**

Appendix: Tax brackets

You can always look up all tax bracket updates at fkianfa.com/updates:
http://fkianfa.com/newsletter/

2018 Ordinary Income Tax Brackets

In 2018, the income limits for all tax brackets and all filers will be adjusted for inflation and will be as follows. The top marginal income tax rate of 37 percent will hit taxpayers with taxable income of $500,000 and higher for single filers and $600,000 and higher for married couples filing jointly.

Marginal Tax Rate	Single	Married Filing Jointly	Head of Household	Married Filing Separately
10%	$0-$9,525	$0-$19,050	$0-$13,600	$0-$9,525
12%	$9,525-$38,700	$19,050-$77,400	$13,600-$51,800	$9,525-$38,700
22%	$38,700-$82,500	$77,400-$165,000	$51,800-$82,500	$38,700-$82,500
24%	$82,500-$157,500	$165,000-$315,000	$82,500-$157,500	$82,500-$157,500
32%	$157,500-$200,000	$315,000-$400,000	$157,500-$200,000	$157,500-$200,000
35%	$200,000-$500,000	$400,000-$600,000	$200,000-$500,000	$200,000-$300,000
37%	Over $500,000	Over $600,000	Over $500,000	Over $600,000

2018 Long Term Capital Gain Tax Brackets

Tax Rate	Single	Married Filing Jointly	Head of Household	Married Filing Separately
0%	$0-$38,600	$0-$77,200	$0-$51,700	$0-$38,600
15%	$38,601-$425,800	$77,201-$479,000	$51,701-$452,400	$38,601-$239,500
20%	$425,801 or more	$479,001 or more	$452,401 or more	$239,501 or more

Made in the USA
San Bernardino, CA
28 January 2020

63720310R00095